SUMMER OF '66

SUMMER OF '66

SHELTON L. WILLIAMS

ZONE PRESS
Denton, Texas

SUMMER OF '66
Shelton L. Williams

SECOND EDITION

Published in the United States of America
By Zone Press
an imprint of Rogers Publishing and Consulting, Inc.
201 North Austin
Denton, Texas 76201
info@zonepress.com

Editing and Design: Jim O. Rogers

Photography: Shel Hershorn

Afterword: Gary M. Lavergne

ISBN: 0-9777558-7-8

CONTENTS

INTRODUCTION
AND
ACKNOWLEDGEMENTS

Authors owe a debt of gratitude to many different people. Editors, publishers, and distributors are the critical end of a long chain of support and feedback. In 2003, I began a journey of writing about traumatic personal events that occurred to me in the 1960s. I often say it was a turbulent life in a turbulent time, but we had really great parties! My first book, *Washed in the Blood* (2007), chronicled the infamous Kiss and Kill Murder in Odessa, Texas in 1961.The victim in that event was my cousin, Betty, and her untimely death seared my soul but forty years later compelled me to write about her death, our times, and the effect the two together had on me and whole lot of other people.

I went to the University of Texas in 1962 to escape

Odessa, Betty's tragedy, and trauma they caused. *Summer of '66* demonstrates that not only was I unsuccessful in "putting it all behind," there was more adventure and more reflection ahead. Somehow between 1961 and 1969 I could not avoid being caught up in events that to this day defy explanation. I am not trying to explain Charles Whitman in this book. I can't. I am simply going to recount how his life and mine intersected and I am going to show that there was a lot more going on in Austin that hot summer.

Thanks to my many friends and former students at Austin College who helped me research and write these books. You all deserve a big hug, but a special thanks to Marilyn Bice, my partner and colleague in so many adventures at Austin College for a decade. Your help was indispensable; your energy inexhaustible; and your generosity legendary.

Thank you.

With that said, I dedicate this book to my children, their spouses and my grand children. Greg and Jill (Hunter-Williams) and Becca and David (Collins), I love you. Grayson and Clara Hunter-Williams, all my love. Pops

FOREWORD

Prudence Macintosh, the noted author and Texas icon, is a friend of mine and I thank her for permission to use this speech she made twenty or so years ago at the University of Texas at Austin. I know it is an unusual foreward to a little book about Austin in the Summer of 1966, but in truth it sets the scene for what comes next. In case you are wondering, she mentions a shy, frightened young man from Odessa, Texas. Yes, it is yours truly, so aside from setting the scene for Austin c 1966, it tells you a little bit about the scribbler telling the story afterwards. Here's what Prudence had to say.

UT COMMENCEMENT - May 18, 1985

PRESIDENT FLAWN, DISTINGUISHED GUESTS, EX-STUDENTS, CLASS OF '85 and FACULTY,

It's quite a thrill for me to suit up with you tonight. My degree was conferred with all of the *ceremony the postman in Texarkana could muster. At forty, I'm finally old enough to appreciate the value of traditions. Perhaps by participating in this ceremony I will banish once and for all the dream which plagues all students long beyond their school days — a final exam in a course you never attended. You never bought the text and you can't read the room numbers or the test questions*

I accepted this invitation to speak to you as if I had just stepped off the campus. My assignment looked easy — reminisce about the 60's and 70's. Well, that's just reviewing yesterday's newspapers. Such recent happenings hardly merit the name history. You remember the Cuban missile crisis? It was the only time my parents accepted a collect call from me. Well, at least you remember the Kennedy assassination ... It happened just before Dr. Soukup's 1:00 government class on Friday. We had all laughed with, perhaps at our professors. That day we cried with them too. You weren't even born, were you? I've been away longer than I thought.

The fact is, even though Lynda Bird Johnson and her secret service men, the Powder Puff Patrol, matriculated with us in the early sixties, the real work of the newspaper's front page seldom intruded here. My newspaper father sometimes sent me current Events quizzes in his letters. "Honey, do you know where Yemen is?" he'd ask. No, I didn't, but we had our own microcosm going right here. And for a kid who had grown up in a small town, it didn't seem so micro. I hadn't located Yemen, but I was drinking coffee occasionally in the Chuck Wagon with Hisham Khadumi, and a table full of Arab students. I was doing my bit for Pan American studies by riding in a convertible with Gustavo Vergara from Pueblo, Mexico and Luis Sobral from Brazil. These handsome young men delighted my roommates and me with hilarious parodies of our Anglo dates whom they derisively dubbed, "The Flattops." My roommate for two semesters was Julia Fu Shaw, a Chinese girl who had grown up in Argentina. To keep things going multinationally, she dated a German boy named Hans. Well, for Prudence Mahaffey from Texarkana, just meeting kids from high plains was an exotic experience. Those West Texas women who had grown up with so much sky seemed to me to be a wilder, stronger breed and beside them, I felt positively dainty.

My freshman year I emerged from Gregory Gym with six 8:00 classes — two classes on Saturday including a lab which lasted until noon. I think they saw me coming. I never missed a class. None of you were ever that intimidated. A West Texas boy from Odessa whom I'd met at freshman orientation became my soul mate. We'd pass each other on the drag, exchange panicky looks and ask,

"Surviving?" What made us honor students in our respective small ponds, we quickly discerned was just barely adequate at UT. Another classmate who is now a surgeon in Tyler admits that on his first day here, he unpacked his bags, walked across this mall with a sea of humanity (about half the number you walk with daily,) then hurried back to his room, knelt by his bed and prayed, "Please God, don't let me be average." Well, those of us who were average accepted it with humility and then went on to have some rather extraordinary days here.

All Texas Exes probably think of their particular years as being pivotal in the school's history. I have a certain bias about 1962-66. These were the years of legendary professor! William Arrowsmith, John Silber, Walter Prescott Webb, Roger Shattuck, Irwin Spear, Tom Cranfill. Doc Ayres in the English Dept. was just a kid. To balance all that academic ferment, we also had the longest stint of athletic triumphs UT has ever known. One of my friends used to say he sometimes regretted not going to Stanford, but never on Saturdays. Darrell Royal — the Pope could not have been regarded with greater reverence.

But the times, they were a changin'. Integration was a big issue on campus — as it should have been. We were the last generation who had consciously drunk from separate water fountains and had been taught never to sit at the back of the bus.

Before I graduated, the cowboy minstrels dropped their black faced routines, dorms, barbershops, Roy's Lounge, the movie theaters and athletic teams removed unjust barriers. To the casual observer, the campus probably still looked like a bush league boot camp for Miss Americas. Oh, we had queens and sweethearts for everything — Varsity Carnival, Miss Campus Chest, ROTC sweethearts. My sons have a 1963 photograph of me in the hall between their bedrooms in full military regalia standing in front of an R.O.T.C. plaque which bears the inscription "Of and for the troops." They're still puzzled about what Mommy did in the war. Texans have never seen much point in ignoring an 18 year old female pulchritude, but even the fluffiest bubble head winced a little when a beatnik named Janis Joplin who sang on the Union steps won the Ugly Man contest our sophomore year. The Academic Center opened while I was here as the most glamorous undergraduate library on campus, and there was much talk of a University of the First Class. There began a palpable energy on this campus which I still feel — the image of the big party school was retreating. We may have believed that we were that "first class." It was no longer weird to have a date to the library on Friday nights.

The union brought every speaker imaginable. Tom Wolfe, Truman Capote, Madame Nhu, William Buckeley, Bernard Fall and William Sloane Coffin. Betty Friedan came to our Challenge Colloquium to promote her new book THE FEMININE MYSTIQUE. Stump speakings replete with hecklers foreshadowed the tumultuous decade that would follow mine when just shaving one's legs might be taken for a political statement.

By the time I graduated, a certain idealism was abroad. Some of my classmates went to Biafra to feed starving children. Others joined the Peace Corps which advertised the lowest pay for "the toughest job you'll ever love." The majority of us assuaged our guilt by pricking social consciences wherever we went and by choosing volunteer jobs that had nothing to do with resume enhancement. The late sixties and early 70's deserve their own spokesman. These are the years your parents are glad you missed. I knew the campus then only as a spectator and enjoyed its excesses as one enjoys a carnival. After all, I was only 25 when Abbie Hoffman said, "Don't trust anybody over thirty." But I can't speak with any personal knowledge of the devastation of drugs, the exhilaration and inevitable sadness of the sexual revolution or the self righteousness of the anti-war movement. I was having my first baby the week the students were shot at Kent State and while I recorded the incident in his baby book, as I peered into his omniscient newborn eyes, I could not be anything but optimistic about the world.

If you have been accused of apathy during your student days, it's hard for me to see what anyone expected you to protest. The decade between us eliminated every possible university restriction that might have pinched you personally. Indeed you might have longed for a few curfews and limits now and then. As for the global issues, I'm not sure how one reduces complex issues like the balance of trade or even apartheid in South Africa to slogans on placards. There is still plenty of room for idealism in the world, however. If you're extraordinary, perhaps yours will take the form of keen analytical thinking applied to problems my generation is beginning to shrug over. We need some new thoughts on Mexico. No less important, however, is the one to one literacy teaching going on in branch libraries in my city. To a person the volunteers will tell you that opening the world of the printed page to a fifty year old man or woman is the most rewarding job they've ever had.

I took a lot of things with me in 1966 from this campus. I took some connections. Not until Dr. Weisman's art history course which I took as an elective, did I see that history and music and math and art and philosophy and literature had some connective threads. He gave me the framework for an education that will never be finished. Finding ways to connect hearts and minds — connecting what should be with what is physically or technologically possible is a part of every vocation including mine as mother. It's a life long endeavor. For the record, there is also algebra in adult life. It rears its ugly head about fourteen years after your first child is born.

Of course I took other connections with me as well. I always bristle when I hear any university, especially mine, described as a place to make your contacts in life. The best contact I made was my spouse. We never intended to marry right out of college, but in retrospect we never encountered a better marriage market. You might want to delay your departure tonight until you find somebody. I might also confess that as a writer for "Texas Monthly" it has helped a great deal to know folks from Borger to Brownsville and from Elysian Fields to El Paso. They are my sounding boards and my most hospitable sources. When I first published in "Texas Monthly," UT friends and classmates I hadn't seen in years came out of the woodwork to encourage me. They clipped and mailed pertinent articles, raised provocative questions and became my intimate audience across the country. When

McCall's sent me to write a story about Supreme Court Justice Sandra Day O'Connor in Arizona, I was relieved that I had friends who'd grown up on similar ranches who could explain to me what releathering a well entailed or what a rancher meant when he greeted another rancher with the question, "Burnin' pear?"

Treasure these friends you've made here. Those friendships formed before professional facades and before competitive egos take hold will be a comfort to you in ways you can't imagine.

I hope you have learned humility here as I did, but I also hope you found some encouragement. I certainly never told anyone I wanted to be a writer — not even myself, but my memory holds dear the day my American Lit Professor Anthony Hilfer read my paper on Ring Lardner aloud to the class and said, "That's a find piece of writing."

Even if you were born elsewhere, I don't have to remind you that these four years have probably made you a Texan. Studying in the old humanities reading room in this main building, I sometimes got bored with my books, leaned back in my chair and read the gilt inscriptions on those ornate beams. The quotations ran the gamut from Dante to Alice in Wonderland. It occurred to me that only in Texas would we juxtapose the Angels at Bethlehem saying "Fear Not, for behold I bring you glad tidings of great joy" on a beam with "I shall never retreat or surrender. Victory or death." William Barret Travis at the Alamo. Because we've always done things a little peculiarly and because we have unique resonances in our history, you don't have to swallow every fool trend that a California or New York exports. You don't even have to define yourself in Yuppie magazine surveys. It's your birthright to have a measure of self confidence that the rest of the world may not have. Without that sort of foolhardy confidence, would I have agreed to stand up here tonight?

you have swum in a very large ocean here already without much of a life preserver. You are survivors, and that count: for a lot in this world.

Those of us who swam here before you and survived feel a special bond with you. We will be cheering you on. CONGRATULATIONS.

CHAPTER 1

YAHTZEE SUMMER

The tiny apartment on Rio Grande Street was the perfect place for a young married couple in Austin, Texas in 1966. Barely 600 feet square, it was classified as a "one-bedroom" because it had a partition between its twin beds and an outer room that contained a threadbare couch, a three-person dining table, and a gas-fired stove. In the bedroom a 400-cubic-inch air conditioner designed for a space four times as large blasted artic air directly onto the beds and into the miniscule toilet/shower area. The AC brought the temperature down thirty degrees from the 95 – 100 degree days in the Austin sun. We thought the place was heaven on earth.

Janell and I had been married for two years. We had survived a wedding night automobile accident, my father's antics as he divorced my Mom and then moved to Austin himself, and financial juggling that at one time had us working six jobs between us. Now we had only one job each and I was finished with school. Well, I had to wrap up a summer school German course, but it was proving a snap. Besides, I was basking in the glory of a full scholarship offer from the Johns Hopkins School of Advanced International Studies (SAIS) in Washington, DC. Life was good.

My dad was a little problem, I admit. OK, he was more than that. He was a major irritant. In my memory we had always competed for ego space. I had left my hometown, Odessa, Texas, in 1962 hoping to put him, our car wash business, and West Texas far behind. I chose the University of Texas because I saw my buddy, Kenneth Self, a bench player for the University of Texas football team, on television at some bowl game in January 1961. Self was a smart guy; UT was a good school; and Austin was not in West Texas. So I went. Unfortunately my dad came to Austin the same summer Janell and I got married - 1964. He brought his long-time girlfriend, Dallas Lanier, with him. On a hot and dusty June afternoon he bought a car wash on north Burnett Road where I had found employment as the manager. A few days later he called my mother from our small apartment to tell her that because of a housing shortage in Austin, he and Dallas – he called her Dee – would simply be forced to live together. Mom called back two minutes later to tell him that she'd grant him the divorce for which he'd long been asking.

For years I assumed that she called him back because he and Dee intended to live together. That he called her from my phone with me in the room was the actual reason. She had always known that he and Dee were together. So did I, but I didn't really have to deal with it directly. It was a "secret." Only once, on a memorable trip to Carlsbad Caverns, did I have to be around them on a social occasion. Little did he know that on a typical date in high school I'd cruise by Dee's wide body trailer just to check to see if Daddy's pink Cadillac were parked outside. It usually was. Better there, I thought, than driving the streets of Odessa drunk.

I was always aware that my mother and father weren't a happily married couple. Well, there was that little thing that he was almost never at home. I also knew that he was "with" Dee. Her trailer was on my dad's property; her son, Kirk, always worked for my dad, and Daddy treated him like a second son. My dad's best employee, Grow, a handsome Cajun black guy from Oberlin, LA also kept me updated on my dad's relationship with her. Many years back, she talked Daddy into firing Grow and bringing her in to manage the car wash. It was a disaster as our car wash lost nearly a third of its business. She never quit trying to get rid of him though. Finally Grow quit of his own accord. He went to work for Carl Sewell Ford in Odessa, but he died suddenly my sophomore of college. He suffered from kidney failure. I don't know the details because Daddy never told me that Grow had gone to the hospital. I saw him the month before, however.

"Mark my word, Shelly Bill. That scar-faced bitch

gonna ruin your family," he told me.

I didn't have the heart to tell him. My family was long since ruined.

Since moving to Austin Daddy and Dee had become omnipresent in our lives, especially during the summers. While I quit the employ of the car wash (he hired Dee to replace me as manger), I still could not get away from them. Using the logic that "you always have to eat," they seemed to contact us daily to invite us over for dinner. After we declined several times claiming that we had already eaten, they called earlier and earlier in the afternoon. We established 3:30 PM as the all-time record for saying that we'd already had dinner. Still, they could not be totally avoided.

We had meals with them when forced to. We let my dad "handle" the insurance claim we had as the result of a wedding night car accident caused by a drunken driver. He did a lousy job actually, but he wanted credit for lying to the insurance company about the cost of Janell's wedding dress destroyed in the collision. When we didn't show the proper enthusiasm for his negotiating skills, he sulked and nearly cried as we later sat together in an Austin Mexican food restaurant. He was trying too hard in truth. Dee did as well, since she wanted us to be a "family." I had never had one and I wasn't about to start with them. Truth was: I didn't know what a family was. TV offered many models of no consequence and it was many years later that I realized that those shows were national daydreams rather than reflections of slightly exaggerated reality. My reality made me doubt that any Williams' man, including myself, could produce a happy family. That didn't keep Daddy and Dee from trying to convince Janell and me that a few hot meals and access to a color TV could do it for the four of us.

By 1966 it was almost over. Daddy would never follow us to Washington, DC. When I went to SAIS, we would be rid of the daily pressure forever. Even better, I would be going to a place where being a Democrat was not a horrible thing. To Daddy any political affiliation was anathema. Growing up in Odessa being a Democrat was akin to being a card-carrying Stalinist. At UT, especially in the circles Janell and I frequented, it was simply a step away from being a proto-fascist. Kennedy's assassination, the Civil Rights movement, and especially the Viet Nam War had radicalized our politically active friends. Janell and I understood their angst and we even generally agreed with many of their criticisms, but we seriously doubted that President Johnson had actually personally plotted JFK's assassination or that Viet Nam was solely a ploy to expand business opportunities for the Houston-based and LBJ-connected Brown and Root Construction Firm. These were the issues of the time among our friends, but in the summer of 1966 – to us anyway – they took a backseat to wanton pleasure and carefree hedonism.

No, it wasn't our "Summer of Love." We pretty much had that already. Two years married and in the groove, we were having a very fine time in that little twin bed in

23

front of the thermo-blaster. Sex was not our distraction from escalating war, racial tension, and mounting national despair. Yahtzee was. Sometimes Monopoly. After four years of incredible self-denial, I was ready for games. Did I say self-denial? No dates, no movies, no parties, no TV, and no sports activities for four years. Each day I had made a "things to do" list which included nothing but papers to write, notes to review, or letters to send to a distant fiancée. In four years I had never – never – gone to bed without crossing off as completed every item on the list. I knew a grad school scholarship was impossible without good grades, so, by God, I got them. By the summer of '66, I was ready for Double Yahtzee.

Tony Pate and Mary Ann Wycoff were our co-conspirators in pleasure. Tony, a brilliant student in Political Philosophy, became a constant in our daily struggle to find more ways to waste more time. Reruns of the Dick Van Dyke Show followed by twenty straight games of Yahtzee followed by lunch followed by a marathon game of Monopoly followed by watching a summer replacement show called Hootenany was a typical day. We all played to win, but Tony was particularly intense. "What would Lenin do?" was his usual query when confronted with a critical strategic move. Mary Ann was a pretty brunette and my successor the upcoming year as the President of the Political Science Honors society. She and I often opted out of the games to gossip about the UT Government Department, but Tony and Janell soldiered on. There were purchases to make and then houses and hotels to build on exotic properties like Broadway and Park Place. And we could bash Republicans every step of the way.

It's hard to imagine a more carefree summer and every one of us knew it was a fleeting, yet perfect, moment in time. It was true. We would never again have three months – make that, two months – of such abandon again. What made it even more exciting and led to one of our greatest adventures ever was the day the underwear went missing. That day made the summer. That day board games, TV shows, and departmental politics took a backseat to intrigue. That day we took the first step to "the Mystery Man." That day would forever change our lives.

Shelly and his friend Marzouk at the Villa Rose

CHAPTER II

THE GREAT UNDERWEAR CAPER

Perhaps I should explain about the underwear. It wasn't ours. Janell and I "managed" a twenty-four-unit apartment complex called the Villa Rose. We had become managers simply by deciding to move there. Sam Rosen, an Austin jeweler, owned the place, and he employed older students to look after it since he could not be there on site daily. Tenants filed complaints with us; vending machine men checked in with us; rent checks filled our mailbox on the first of each month; and anyone whose white cotton underwear disappeared reported it to us. Since Janell and I handled these trivial managerial duties, Sam graciously lowered our month's rent from $85 a month to $65 a month. With that discount and my new job, Janell and I could take classes at UT and we could afford to live at the Rose my senior year.

Don and Ray Harris lived in the last unit on the south end of the first floor. We lived on the second

27

floor in the middle unit over the vending machines and laundry room next to the stairs. Our unit was isolated and freestanding. No loud neighbors were adjacent. Don and Ray were quiet and well behaved down there on the far end of the first floor. They had been at the Rose for a semester and part of the summer, but we barely knew them. They were business majors, not politicos, and their khaki pants, buttoned- down madras shirts, and nice brown loafers suggested money. I had no real interest in knowing them, but well-behaved tenants were a blessing, so I bore neither any ill will.

Janell was in the kitchen when the boys knocked. I was at my early morning German class. The awkwardness of the moment was more or less fleeting. The boys were there to report that their entire collection of white cotton briefs had been pilfered and a young, curvaceous woman wearing no shoes and a pair of shorts answered the door.

"Hello, Guys," she said.

"Oh, hi, Janell, we're Don and Ray Harris from downstairs," Ray, the older, said.

"Sure," she replied, "How are ya?" She didn't ask them in because I wasn't there and because, really, there was no room for them to sit comfortably.

"We're OK," Ray said, "but...but..."

"Somebody stole our shorts," Don blurted out.

Ray recovered. "Yes, that's right. We have to report a theft, I suppose."

Shortly thereafter the three of them were searching

the laundry and vending machine rooms for ten pairs of jockey briefs. The comical nature of the predicament tickled Janell, and she took extra delight in the boys', especially Ray's, discomfort at dealing with her instead of me.

"So, you're sure they were stolen?" she teased. "You didn't just forget where you last took them off?"

"This doesn't have anything to do with the frat party last night, does it?"

"For the police report, could you explain explicitly how much elastic was in the legs of those panties?"

Janell is from West Texas. Don and Ray were from Houston. Ray was bit nonplussed by her directness and her teasing, but Don loved it.

"The only thing I am sure of is that I wasn't wearing them when they disappeared," he chuckled.

"You sure?" she continued.

Looking inside his pants, Don said, "Pretty sure." Ray was visibly uncomfortable by the banter, so he launched into the story. The underwear had been in the washing machine while the boys retreated to their apartment, "to study," he emphasized. Twenty or thirty minutes later when they came back to check, the machines were empty. Water covered the floor. It seems someone just took them right out of the wash and walked away.

Janell loves a mystery. Just about any mystery will do, and she is not above concocting one where none exists. In our previous apartment building where we were the tenants and another couple managed it, the wife vanished a few weeks after we moved in. Janell immediately assumed that the guy had chopped her up and buried her in the weeds behind the complex. I protested that interpretation, but my contention that they had simply broken up or that she had been called away on some family emergency failed to impress Janell, as the guy never mentioned her again. Initially he seemed to suggest that we'd be seeing each other as couples, but he never said a word about it – or her – again. Janell took strolls behind the apartments to see if she could catch a whiff of an odor, but while the corpse never materialized, Janell never let go of her theory either. She simply altered where she thought the body might be stashed.

She contended: "I know when girls are about to ditch a guy. I can tell. That girl was happy and she was in love with being in love. He got rid of her. I know it."

After a year, the woman never showed up, but then neither did the police. Janell simply said that proved how clever and fiendish he actually was. I had already learned that it was pointless to argue why something had not happened. In any event the "case of the missing underwear" did not seem at first glance to be as exciting as a chopped up spouse, but it was a mystery nevertheless.

She intended to solve it.

Chapter III

Night Work

In 1966 I was one of two night watchmen at the Texas Department of Health Bureau of Vital Statistics. Among other things, birth and death records were stored there. Before I got the cushy night watchman's job, I had worked four hours a day at the Bureau pulling, copying, and laminating such records. In down times, the college boys who worked there looked up the records of the famous and the infamous. LBJ's birth record. Lee Harvey Oswald and Jack Ruby's death records. We delighted in the mistakes and misspellings. President's Kennedy's last address was listed as 600 Pennsylvania Ave instead of 1600 Pennsylvania Ave. Governor Hogg did not have two daughters named Ima and Ura. Silly things like that. It was boring, but I consoled myself with thoughts that some great political figures had started in such mundane surroundings. LBJ had been a teacher. Mao had once worked as a library assistant. The great scholar and diplomat, George

F. Kennan, had grown up on a farm. Maybe I had a great future, I speculated, because my first job was equally as humble as these great movers and shakers.

My second post with the Bureau as night watchman was equally as boring, but it had special benefits. For one thing, I could study on the job. Most importantly, it paid $220 a month since it was forty hours a week. I worked every other night from 11:00 PM until 6:00 AM and then twenty-five or twenty-six hours over the weekend depending on the days I worked. On weekends when I pulled the shift from Saturday at noon until Sunday at 1:00 PM, Janell would join me around 6:00 PM. Much to the delight of the firemen at the fire station across from the Bureau, this sweet thing would park in front of the building and make trip after trip into the Bureau bringing our laundry, the ironing board, hot food, blankets and pillows. Oh, and the portable TV. Our white '61 Ford Fairlane became a welcome sight to the fearless firefighters, and I watched from the Bureau's door as they congregated at the front of the fire station at first glimpse of it.

She slept at the Bureau most Saturday nights. Actually we both slept. I was not in fact much of a night watchman. I never walked any "rounds" in the cavernous Bureau's halls. The building had four floors above ground and below a huge basement where the records were stored. At night, all of these places were dark, ominous, and, as far as I was concerned, unapproachable. No one told me to check each floor during the night, or if they did, it didn't register with me. Instead when I came in at 11:00 PM just as the all male black cleaning crew was leaving, I went directly to the Health Director's plush office, spread out my foam rubber pad on his carpeted floor, locked his door, placed a cracked Jackie Jensen baseball bat within easy reach, and went straight to sleep. The fellow, Bob Rothberg, who alternated nights with me took a slightly different approach. Bob was a law student, and he studied all night long. He did not do rounds either, but he carried a German Lugar. Neither one of us ever encountered a prowler the year we served the State of Texas, but many a night I found myself standing in the lobby, bat in hand, obviously reacting to a noise that had disturbed my fitful slumber. No one was ever there. No sound emanated from the dark at the end of the hall or from the creepy blackness at the top of the first set of stairs just a few feet from the Bureau's front door.

Nothing ever moved me to take the elevator to the fourth floor during the night, and only rarely, and only in broad daylight and in the presence of others, would I ever take the ladder from the fourth floor to the storage attic just above it. It may have been reasonable to expect a night watchman to do these things and go to these places, but I had no intention of exploring the unlit corners or spooky halls of Austin's finest government building on 5th Street. Instead, we referred to my job as Shelly's "Health Department Scholarship."

Later that summer I would definitely earn that scholarship.

Chapter IV

The Mystery Man

Janell spent a lot of time alone that summer. I was in class every weekday morning and I was gone for huge portions of Saturday and Sunday every weekend. On occasion she would even ignore the Yahtzee games as she got the "Hollis Bug" to clean and straighten the apartment. Hollis was Janell's maiden name and her mom had meticulously cleaned and cared for every one of the multitudes of tiny rent houses and motel rooms that her father, a grocery man and gypsy, had moved them into and out of in various West Texas towns. Thus, Janell moved several times a year growing up, but her mother kept every place tidy, even the ratty duplex on Brentwood Drive in Odessa where she was living when we met and fell in love my senior year of high school. So periodically Janell cleaned and straightened every one of the 600 square inches of our apartment at the Rose.

But she was happier and healthier than she had ever

been in her life. She loved Austin. She loved school. And, with my Mom's help, she had discovered and corrected the anemia that had made her so tired and lethargic the previous couple of years. Bright, well, and sexy as hell, she felt right at home in Austin. And now she had a mystery to solve!

The time alone allowed her the opportunity to think through the events of the summer. The Rose's coke machines started running out too quickly and not enough money was deposited in them. The girl three doors down from Don and Ray reported a Peeping Tom. Janell heard a shuffling sound on the stairway one night shortly after I left for work at the Bureau. Little but unusual things were happening.

"There's someone in these apartments doing all this," she concluded.

"Why do you think it's someone from the Rose?" I asked.

"No one has seen this person. How can someone haul cokes and underwear or peek and run away without ever being seen coming or going?" she retorted.

"How can you be sure he's not been seen?" I wondered.

"He or she," Janell responded.

Janell was eighteen years old when we got married. She was from a poor, fundamentalist, and not terribly educated family. Got the stereotype? Now forget it. She was clever, independent, and assertive from day one. She

36

had never asked me for permission to do anything and she had not even mentioned to me that she had already begun an investigation into the incidents at the Rose. In fact the investigation was in its third week. Not only had she talked to other tenants, the coke man, and the neighbors across the street, she had knocked on the door of the fraternity house situated only a few feet from the apartment complex. We officially hated fraternities. We even refused to learn the name of the one right next door. That did not prevent us from occasionally lying on the deck in front of our second story apartment and, through the frat house's large plate glass window, watch the revelers on a Friday or Saturday night. Neither of us admitted that they looked like fun since we were so much more mature and intellectual than the Greek jerks we were watching. But I digress.

"How could you have gone to the frat house?" I wondered.

"The two guys I talked to were actually nice," she said.

"Nice? Of course, they were nice. A gorgeous girl appears out of nowhere at the front door, of course they'll be nice," I said.

"Don't be silly. They hardly noticed me. You have seen those pretty sorority girls all made up and rich," she contended. "They probably felt sorry for me."

To this day when a friend or colleague calls her movie star pretty, she denies, declines, or derides the notion. Here she was probably dressed early Hippie, peasant blouse and long straight hair. And did I mention the curves? Right, the frat boys didn't notice her.

"OK, forget what they thought of you," I said, "What did they say about the Peeping Tom. My guess is it was one of them."

"No, they were genuinely concerned, but they haven't seen or heard anything," she responded. "My working assumption is that he's from right here."

"Or she," I quickly interjected.

"No, I have thought about it. Men's underwear went missing. The girl was leaving the shower and..."

"Maybe a butch lesbian," I pressed half-heartedly.

"Yeah," she said, "I thought about that, but a woman would not have watched her in the shower. She would have picked a more meaningful event, like when she was combing her hair or lying stretched out on the bed. This was a typical horny guy."

Note to self. Figure out women some day.

I assumed it was a guy too, but no thought had gone into it. Still I had no idea whether he – we came to call him "The Mystery Man" – lived at the Rose or not. I sure hoped not. But then I also assumed that the few minor incidents we had witnessed would not last long and it'd all be over before we left town in mid-August. Janell disagreed. She said that this was just the beginning.

As usual, she was right, and I was wrong.

A calm and peaceful Tower, Shel Hershorn

Chapter V

Busted I

He was huddled against the wall, bent over, and slightly shaking. Janell could see him as a reflection in the frat house plate glass window. He was a skinny teenager wearing cut-off jeans shorts and a torn white T-shirt. He was not peering around the wall. Instead he was balled up, head down, hoping to avoid discovery. Janell's mistake was to stop walking naturally, simply to stop to observe the Mystery Man cowering in the early morning sun along side his favorite vending machine room. After a few seconds he realized that she had come to a stop. He listened briefly and then suddenly realized that his position along the wall was too far forward. His reflection was clearly visible in the glass. A quick turn of the head toward the plate glass confirmed his worse fear, but it also allowed Janell to see the pimply face beneath his dirty blonde hair. He was eighteen, maybe nineteen. When their eyes met, Janell's first instinct was to walk forward toward him. He obviously had no weapon. His reaction, conversely, was to turn and run.

As he bolted, Janell ran to where he had been crouching. As she rounded the corner, he was maybe thirty feet away running through the backyard of the abandoned Victorian house next to the Rose. There was no fence and the overgrown yard was strewn with old boards and soggy cardboard boxes. His dirty, once white, sneakers easily avoided the obstacles as he ran through the yard onto the next street and then out of Janell's sight. She was not about to chase him. Instead she began carefully to inspect his hiding place for possible clues or missing items. She really found nothing interesting or revealing, except perhaps a shoe print and an automobile tire iron. Was the tire iron a weapon? No, probably not, she thought, probably a handy tool for jimmying coke machines.

Now the Mystery Man had a face.

CHAPTER VI

CHARLEY FINGERNAILS

The Mystery Man had a face but no name and no background.

"He looks like a smaller version of that guy you told me about, Honey," said Janell that night.

"What guy?" I asked.

"The one on Tuesdays and Thursdays when you were taking the American Political History class, the one who chewed his fingernails," she explained.

"Oh, really, the blonde guy with the burr cut? " I wondered.

"Yeah, that one. What was his name?"

"Never got his name, for sure. Charles, maybe. I heard someone call him Charley, I think," I said. "Why does he come to mind?" I inquired.

"You know the day I ran all the way over to the Architecture Building to tell you about your scholarship?" she asked.

"Sure, I'll never forget. It was around the fifth anniversary of Betty's death and it was the first day I ever saw your face so red."

"Yes, and it was the day I saw that guy you had told me about. I knew it was the fingernails guy but he wasn't chewing them. He was flustered, upset, I thought, because of a grade on a test. He was standing legs akimbo in the middle of the hall glaring at this bluebook and muttering obscenities," she said.

"OK, so?" I asked.

"The look on his face was the same as the Mystery Man's, but as similar as they are, I don't think it's the same guy."

"You said he was smaller, right?" I asked.

"Yes, smaller and certainly not as well dressed," she replied. "The Mystery Man looked a mess while Charley Whoisits was kinda neat. There's one more thing," she said.

"OK, I'll bite, what?" I asked.

"No ring. The Mystery Man was not wearing a wedding ring," she replied.

"So, there's no connection," I said, "except for a similar haircut and a troubled look."

"There is a connection!" she insisted.

Frankly, talking about Charley made me nervous. I wanted to be rid of that guy and his memory, and I had never even exchanged a word with him in my life. But on every Tuesday and Thursday of the spring semester of my senior year, I saw him. We seemed to share a compulsion about being early for class. I had told Janell about his habit of chewing his fingernails seemingly down to the quick, but I hadn't told her the rest. He was a talker, a big talker, and what he said made me nervous. Sometimes he'd just stand there waiting for class, but usually he'd talk to this one friend of his who seemed to hang on his every word, like he was a fan more than a friend.

The guy was a Marine or had been. He was also a hunter. He liked guns. Snippets of conversation would come my way.

"In Nam, I'd be a sniper, man, not a rat fucker."

"What's a rat fucker, Charley?" asked the sycophant.

"They go down into holes looking for Charley. You know, gooks, Communists," he said. "I'd be in the trees picking those bastards off. That's what the Corps trained me to do."

"You going to Viet Nam and kill Charley, Charley?" his friend laughed.

"Oh, hell no, I am finished with the Marines. They can kiss my red, white and blue ass," he said.

The classroom emptied and I gladly went in. The guy made me nervous. He looked like the All American Boy, but he was edgy. Besides, a hunter had killed my cousin Betty five years ago. At close range with a shotgun. At the time it happened people all over town said they could not believe this nice all American Boy, athlete and honors student, could kill his girlfriend in such a cold-blooded way. Every time I heard this Charley guy tell a Marine story or brag about killing a deer and dressing it out in his dorm room shower stall, I had the same reaction. Maybe no one could imagine Mack Herring killing Betty Williams, but they had better not say that about this Charley guy if anything happens. He's seems about to explode.

Janell didn't know that part. She might have a predilection for murder mysteries, but I thought whack jobs were lurking everywhere. My cousin's death my junior year of high school had made me doubt everyone and everything. The class president was probably a crook. The rich lawyer probably manipulated the truth. Good girls were hypocrites and bad girls were ... Well, I wasn't sure what a bad girl was. Several incidents at UT had made me even more wary. A fight I had in intramural basketball that came out of nowhere. A professor's brother who had been murdered while cavorting with a prostitute in a local motel. Two girls had been taken from their swank UT dorm and murdered. The country was falling apart. I had come to expect "bad things." It was odd that this summer of rest and regeneration would be interrupted by Charley Fingernails' memory. I was glad to be rid of him, his smarmy buddy, and his unfunny stories of death and destruction.

Surely Charley Fingernails was not connected to the Mystery Man. Was he?

CHAPTER VII

BAD THINGS

Bad things. I wished to hell that radio and TV had not been invented two days after my birthday in 1966. On July 15, 1966, radio, TV, and the newspaper all reported that Richard Speck had broken into a nurses' dormitory in Chicago and viciously murdered eight student nurses. He had not only murdered them, he had tortured, defiled, and savaged them over the course of a terror-filled night. It was immediately hailed as a new "The Crime of the Century." More bad news from our perspective. Richard Speck, with the "Born to Raise Hell" tattoo on his arm, grew up in Dallas, Texas. Just three years earlier, "Dallas" had killed Kennedy. Now it had butchered innocence in Chicago.

"My God," I said, "what must the world think of us, of Texas?" I whined to Janell. "Another murderer from Texas. And this one the worst yet."

"What are you talking about?" Janell retorted. "How can anyone think anything about Texas because of these incidents? Nuts are everywhere. Besides Albert Desalvo was from Boston. Charles Starkweather was from where? Nebraska? Kansas? Ed Gein, the guy Norman Bates from Psycho is based on, was from Wisconsin. Does anyone blame those places?"

Yes, Janell knew about all these freaks. She was a Psychology major and the seemingly new phenomenon of serial killers fascinated her. She loved Jack the Ripper movies as a kid (especially the 1959 British version) and she loved tales of unsolved multiple slayings. She even watched Psycho with her eyes open. I know. She told me about the shower scene I couldn't watch. However, I couldn't stand such stories. Even as a child I could not watch "scary" movies and the fear persisted later into my life. I remember as a teen abandoning my buddies without a ride home at a drive-in theater just on the eastern outskirts of Odessa so I would not have to watch a re-release of The Thing, a laughably unscary movie that had frightened me as a six-year-old. (Yes, I saw it much later in life.) Anyway, she knew about these things and I manifestly did not. Thus, my next question to her was:

"Who is Albert DeSalavia?"

"Desalvo, dummy. The Boston Strangler. The guy who'd pretend to be some kind of official to gain entry into women's homes and then brutalize them. Killed twelve of them"

"Starkweather?" I asked.

"He and Caril Fugate," she replied, "went on a wild

killing spree in Nebraska in 1958. Killed 14-15 people. He was nineteen; she was fifteen."

"Wow. OK," I said. "I get your point, but it seems like Texas has more than its share of violence and killing. Or at least the news sources act like it does."

"I know, Honey, but you are a social scientist. You know this isn't an isolated phenomenon and you know there's more focus on Texas now because LBJ is from Texas and a lot of folks are unhappy with Viet Nam. They are personalizing their political preferences."

I knew that, but even then I tended to focus on the issues and the policy arguments rather than the personalities. Immaturely, I thought it was unfair to blame Texas or Texans for Kennedy's death. Kennedy had been my inspiration and I was from Texas. It made no difference that LBJ was from Texas. His arguments were wrong. That's all. Dean Rusk, his Secretary of State, was from Georgia, not Texas. Robert McNamara, his Secretary of Defense, was from Michigan, not Texas. Besides, Kennedy, from Massachusetts, appointed them all. It upset me that news stories seemed to focus on Texas as some sort of malevolent place. As a young man I didn't want unfairness. I didn't want serial killers. I didn't want death and destruction. I didn't want the place I lived in to be widely perceived as the home of deranged killers. Nevertheless, I had come to expect bad things. I wanted no more to do with "the Mystery Man" or Charley Fingernails.

"Honey," Janell said, disturbing my distracted reverie. "I saw him again today."

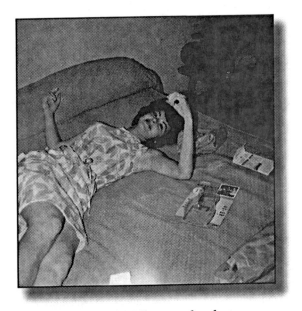

Janell Williams, sleuth

Chapter VIII

My Wife, The Sleuth

"Who'd ya see?" knowing the answer to the question before I asked it.

"The Mystery Man," she said excitedly. "He was coming out of Cabel's Minit Mart just as I was coming out of the card shop across the street on 30th. Oh, that reminds me, I have your birthday card. It's only two days late this time."

"Tell me about the guy," I said impatiently and ignoring the card. "Did he see you? What was he doing at the store? Did anything happen?"

"Not at the store," she said, almost quietly.

"What? What do you mean 'not at the store'? Did something happen somewhere else? Did he see you?" I was agitated, and she knew it.

"No," she said, "Shelly, calm down. He did not see me. He never saw me, but, uh, I sorta followed him."

"You what?" I almost exploded. "You followed this monster."

"Whoa, wait a minute," she said. "Who says he's a

monster? All we know is petty stuff. He's a coke thief. Big Deal. Besides, I think I am starting to figure him out."

"What the hell do you mean, figure him out? No, wait, where did you follow him? Are you sure he never saw you?" I wondered.

"You're not going to believe this, Honey. I followed him next door to us," she said.

She saw the questions in my eyes, so she went on. "He walked part of the way down the alley behind Cabell's. He cut through between those little houses across the street. He crossed Rio Grande. Walked between the Rose and the frat house and headed for the back door of that old Victorian house right next door, across that lot. He's staying there, I know he is."

"You know no such thing," I said.

"Well, yes, I think I do. He took his sweet rolls and candy into the house, but first he looked this way and that before he went in. He didn't see me because if he had, he would have taken off. He doesn't want anyone to know he's in there. But, I know," she smiled at her clever sleuthing.

"Too many assumptions," I responded. "How do you know he had sweet rolls and candy? How do you know he didn't see you? How do you know he is staying there and not just hiding stuff there temporarily?"

"Not bad, Mr. Phi Beta Crapa, but nothing beats on-the-ground research," she retorted.

"Huh?"

"One," she said, "I know it was sweet rolls and

candy because I went back to Cabell's and asked if they had been having any petty thefts. I told them that we had been losing cokes and I wondered if they had losses as well. I know grocery people, and guess what?"

"Sweet rolls and candy are missing," I took a wild guess.

"Yes," she said. "I was already pretty sure because I saw the sun reflected on the tin as he carried it."

"Control yourself, Agatha Christie," I said. "And you know he didn't see you because…?"

"Well, as I followed him, someone walked out of one of the houses he was near, and he almost freaked. He is averse to being seen by other people. He damned near jumped out of his skin. If he had seen me, he would have reacted. He is a scared little boy," she said.

"I am not convinced," I said. "And how do you know he's living in the house? And don't tell me you did something dangerous."

"No, no way," she said. "I watched the house from our apartment window, and I didn't go in until I saw him go out again."

"Holy Mother of God, you went in!" I did explode.

"Wait, wait," she said. "I didn't go "in" in. I just went in the backdoor a bit and I saw some of the stuff. I saw a candy wrapper and a piece of cellophane. It made something of a trail to the stairs and …"

"That's it. Tell me that you did not go up the stairs," I said.

"I did not go up the stairs," she said.

"Honor Bright?" I inquired. We have a solemn commitment never to lie on Honor Bright.

"Honor bright," she said. "Besides I thought I heard something out back, so I went out the front door."

"You are kidding me, right?" I implored. "None of this happened, right?"

"Baby, we agreed always to tell the truth in our marriage. It all happened just that way," she said as if that would reassure me. "He's probably harmless."

"Another assumption," I asserted.

"Requiring more research," she retorted.

"No way. Honey, you cannot go alone into this house with a guy whose behavior is damned strange, as it is. He might be a homeless waif or he might be the next Richard Speck. You just can't do it. Please." This time I really was imploring.

She paused a moment and it seemed that she was actually contemplating what I had said. She could understand the urgency in my plea. She wanted to be as safe as I did. I assumed.

"OK, Honey, I promise that I will never go into that house alone again. But I will gather more clues. OK?" She smiled sweetly and moved closer. I knew there was no real stopping what she called "research."

"OK," I said, knowing full well that somehow I had just been had.

Chapter IX

Equals

"Honey," I said, "do you believe in marriage?"

"No, but I believe in our marriage," she said.

Thus, we decided not to get divorced and just live together. It was the '60s; social revolution was all around us and in our early twenties, we weren't entirely sure how to react. We settled on striving toward having an equal partnership and reviewing the state of that partnership every five years. Maturity, jobs, children, crises and the times we have lived through altered the way we talk about the meaning of marriage in our lives, but forty years later we stick to that five-year review. Periodically one of us will joke that something the other wants or needs is "not in our original contract," but the commitment to an equal partnership remains intact. In the summer of 1966, I learned quite a few lessons about what "equal" means.

Tony and Mary Ann had just left for the evening. The Monopoly game had been less spirited than usual, but the banter had been lively enough. Tony, for all of his philosophical acuity, declared himself no fan of the films of Ingmar Bergman or Federico Fellini. While I did not claim to understand everything in either *Wild Strawberry* or *8 ½,* I defended both movies and both directors vigorously. Tony easily put me on the defensive by saying that the films actually had no real depth and that the directors had a superficial understanding of Philosophy. They were, purely and simply, pseudo-intellectual, as far as Tony was concerned. Their symbolism was heavy-handed and simplistic. Such arguments undid me usually. I liked the films and I found them thought provoking. Who was I to declare them intellectually inferior? What rankled Janell was that in such debates I assumed that Tony was qualified to make such judgments. Normally she would have jumped into the debate to ask Tony exactly who was the pseudo-intellectual and who was the genius in a contest between a college student and Ingmar Bergman, but tonight she didn't weigh in. I expected her to start up with me the second Tony and May Ann left the apartment, asking me why I didn't have more confidence in my own judgment, asserting that it was obvious that Tony had either not seen or had not paid attention to the movies, or something... Instead she stayed quiet and, I thought, a little somber.

"Honey," I said, "Am I wrong about Fellini?"

"Who?" she asked blankly.

"What do you mean, 'Who?' You have sat right there listening to me debate Tony back and forth about

Fellini and Bergman for over an hour."

"Sorry," she said, "maybe I am a little distracted tonight."

"Why?" I asked. "You feelin' OK?"

"Yeah, I'm fine. What time is it? Don't you take off for work soon?"

That was the deal. She was waiting for a time not too long before I took off for the night watchman's job to tell me what was going on. She knew how I'd react and she knew what I'd say when I found out why she was two degrees off plumb, as we'd say in West Texas. She was wise to wait until the last minute. When I told her I had twenty minutes before I left for work, she asked me to sit down.

"I kinda did something dangerous today," she started.

That didn't bother me since she was obviously OK. Close calls are no calls in my book.

"Yeah? What?" I said almost casually.

"Well, you know you told me not to go into that old house alone, right?" she continued.

"Uh oh, yeah?" I said.

"I went in today, but not alone," she answered. "I had protection"

"Protection? What, a weapon? What?" Concern prevailed over anger at this point.

"Yes, well, I did take a knife, but…"

"A knife! A knife!"

"Don't worry, I never needed it. Don had one too," she confessed.

"What, you mean you went in there with Don? Why, I don't understand?" Maybe I'd skip anger and go straight to hurt.

"Yeah, well, Don and I have been kinda hanging out talking about the situation and we started tracking the 'Mystery Man's' coming and going and I have it down really well now. He leaves the house shortly after 9:00 AM, and he doesn't come back there until late afternoon. He waits until people in the neighborhood have gone to work in the morning and returns just before they come home in the afternoon."

"You and Don have observed this?" I didn't ask when, how or where they had done this observing.

"Well, mostly I have, but Don helped and today we went in to see what was going on in that house."

"That's not scary, Honey, that's nuts," I declared.

"Look, it happened, OK? Get over it. What we need to focus on is what Don and I found in that house. Honey, you may be right. The world has a lot of 'bad things' in it."

I left for work that night more distressed than anytime since Betty had died. I was not ready for what Don and Janell had to report. I was not ready for what was about to happen to us. The "Mystery Man" was no innocent, lost teenager, and perhaps neither was Janell nor I.

Janell and Shelly before the revolution

Chapter X

Paper Dolls

A million questions raced in my mind. Why did she go in with Don? Well, he was around, available, as it were. How long had they been hanging around each other? Did that matter as long as they were just friends? Why did she pick him to protect her and not me? That's obvious. I would never have gone in that house. I would have never spied on the 'Mystery Man'? Why wouldn't I? That was the hardest one for me. Since my cousin Betty had died, had I lost my sense of adventure? I had been a grind in undergraduate school. Our marriage was "fine," but over the last couple of months we had been having fun really for the first time. Janell and, come to think of it, I as well, had actually begun to smile more. Regardless of the "bad things" in the world and regardless of the stress, work, and being the perfect student, I had no excuse for becoming boring. These thoughts roiled in my brain, but over-riding them all was what to make of what Janell and Don had found in that house. I could fix my personality and perhaps my relationship later.

"When we went in, the place just looked abandoned," Janell said. I called her when I got to work and I was sitting in the Director's Office of the Bureau of Vital Statistics. I had turned on every light on the first floor of the building, but it proved not to be nearly enough.

"Don went in first," she said.

"How gallant," I interjected.

"Hush. He went in first but as we walked into the foyer, there was nothing. The living room was empty. There were no signs of anything or anyone."

"You should've left then," I said.

"Let me tell this!"

"OK, OK"

"Well, there were stairs. We saw a plastic wrapper on the stairs, and we knew we had to go up there."

I had not watched the shower scene in *Psycho* primarily because of a prior scene involving the stairs. Martin Balsam, a nice guy actor, the kind who usually doesn't die in movies, walks up a flight of stairs in an old, creepy Victorian house, and at the top of the stairs, a knife-wielding psycho appears out of nowhere to plunge the knife into his chest. What about this scene had Janell not understood? Had Don gone first? Could they hear the music from *Psycho* in their minds as they took one tentative step after another? I did not interrupt her again.

"It was scary, Honey, almost like that scene in Psycho."

"Yeah, I remember it."

"But upstairs there was nothing either," she said. "There were several large rooms, probably bedrooms, but, except for some old boards and scraps of paper, they were all empty."

"Go on."

"We found a ladder to the attic."

"Jesus! You didn't."

"Well, Don didn't."

"What?"

"At first, he thought there was no reason to look, but I wanted to see for sure. There was no sound at all. The place was empty."

Except for the soft breathing of an ax-wielding mass murderer cowering against the wall just next to the attic opening, I thought.

"So I went up."

"Nothing there?" I wished out loud.

"Honey, I have never seen anything like it. It was a little hard for my eyes to adjust at first. I just had a sense of paper or papers strewn all over the place. It looked like an attic where old magazines had been stored but all the pages had come undone.

Not what I expected to hear. "Oh really, messy huh?"

"Then my eyes adjusted and I could see a lot more. There were empty bottles of coke, empty sweet roll tins and this sort of makeshift cot over in the corner."

"He's sleeping there, "I said. I thought it would be helpful to point out the obvious. "But what's with the magazine pages?"

"He's not just messy, Honey, he's sick," she said.

"Why? What?"

"Those pages from the magazines were all from girlie magazines, 'Playboy,' Swedish health mags, even 'Glamour'," she said.

"Oh man," I said, "our boy has a problem. OK, as a teenager I had all those magazines in my house, too, but that had all been cleverly hidden in the back corner of my closet.

"No, Honey, he didn't just have these magazines. They were cut up."

"They were cut out of the magazines?" I asked.

"No, they were cut up. Honey, he has carefully mutilated each and every one of those hundreds of pictures of women. Each is different. He has scissored the head off of one. Cut the hand off another. Ripped the legs off this one. Cut the section out that would have the vagina of that one."

I was stunned. I had been right. This guy was dangerous and my baby had been exposed to real peril. She was still in danger. This animal lived next door. What if he had seen them? Who would he go after? The tall guy who had never seen him or the vulnerable young woman who had eyeballed him and invaded his lair? Those pictures? Mutilated women? Was he peeking in girls' windows for sexual titillation or was he picking a victim? Did he know Janell? Did he know I left her alone every other night between 11:00 PM and 6:00 AM? Did Don? That was wrong to think. Could we do anything about this? All of this hit me in an instant.

"You think he saw you leave?" I asked.

"I don't think so," she said softly.

CHAPTER XI

YOU THINK I'M NUTS?

I had no idea where to turn. Perhaps to the Police, but the "Mystery Man" was obviously psychologically unbalanced, so perhaps the place to start would be the Psychological Counseling Services of the University. I thought about asking for a personality transplant while I was in there. I found myself looking everywhere on the UT campus. I had no idea. No fellow student I had known had ever sought out such help. We had no famous incidents of troubled students hurling themselves from the top of the Tower, as had occurred in 1961. The Cuban Missile Crisis in '62 had created considerable trauma, but I recalled no school psychiatrist coming forward to offer us sage advice of how to study for our Biological lab practicals while worrying about the complete destruction of mankind. I figured a large place like UT must have such Mental Health services, however, and I figured Mystery Man was surely a current or former UT student, so maybe that's where I should begin. A few inquiries at the Student Union led me to the campus Directory and then on to the Student Health Center. That turned out to be an old building very close to the Tower itself. "Fitting," I thought.

The Tower. Even in 1966 folks nation-wide had an image of UT athletics, the burnt orange jerseys of the football team, the fight song, and the pretty girls on campus, but those of us on campus viewed the Tower as the symbol of UT life. Its 307-foot presence in the middle of the "forty acres" dominated the landscape. One could never not see the Tower from your dorm, intramural field, stroll between classes, or seat at the football game. A football victory was not complete until the Tower lit up orange, from the top part only for a mere victory over Baylor to the entire building when we won over the hated Aggies. Beyond athletics, the Tower housed the Registrar's office, some of the Teaching Assistants' offices, a portion of the library, and frankly I don't know what else. Sometimes it was an annoying obstacle to getting from one spot to another and sometimes it was the place you took visitors to see the panoramic view of Austin from the observation deck.

From the first day on campus, however, every student also knew it was the launching pad for the occasional suicide leap to death for a troubled peer. Somewhat afraid of heights, I never entered it without thinking of falling – not jumping - from it. I had written most of my Government honors thesis in a carrel high up in the Tower, but I tried never to look out its windows.

As a freshman and sophomore I even refused to look up as the carillon bells rang out show tunes at approximately the noon hour. Note to self: stop being afraid of ordinary things. When I went looking for Student Health Services, I had to cut through the building from west to east to get to what looked like temporary barracks where the Student Services were located on the other side. I called it "going into the dungeon" and I moved quickly through.

When I found the Student Health Services building, I didn't know where to look or with whom to talk. Calling ahead never occurred to me. As a typical student, I assumed one showed up to see a professor or staff person and they ushered you right in. It took a while to find the third floor office of Dr. Maurice Dean Heatly, University psychiatrist, but find it I did. At approximately 2:00 PM on a July afternoon, I walked up the steps to approach the Doctor's office and much to my shock standing there was the guy I hoped never to see again: Charley Fingernails! He was in an agitated state, but he was alone – no fan club in sight. He paced outside the doctor's office. There was no going into that office without passing Charley. Was he about to go in? Should I leave and come back later – much later considering the amount of anxiety he exhibited. I was about to turn to go back down the steps when Charley saw me and, to my horror, seemed to recognize me.

"Hey," he said.

"Hey," I said. "Is this Dr. Heatly's office?"

Damn, I thought, *I hope he doesn't think I think*

he's nuts and needs Dr. Heatly's care. But, then, why was I there? Would he think I was nuts? There was a stigma in 1966 about these matters, and I didn't want him to think ill of me.

"I need to ask him some advice about a Psychology course my wife wants to take," I lied.

"You married?" he asked.

"Yeah"

"Me too," he said. "It's great, isn't it?

What do you know, Charley? Have you heard about Don and my wife? You big, tough Marine, you take care of your wife, don't you? No reason to worry about being a total bore for you. She must get tired of your fingernail chewing though.

"Yeah, great," I said. "Uh, you waiting to see the Doc?" I started to suggest that perhaps his wife wanted course counseling as well, but I let it go.

"No, man, no, I guess not. Go on in. He's an OK guy for a dumb fuck shrink."

"Right," I laughed as if I knew what dumb fuck shrinks were like.

Charley walked past me on his way to the stairs. *How weird was that? I come to see the Doc about the Mystery Man and Charley shows up. Why had he not gone in? Why was he agitated? What kept bringing Charley and the Mystery Man into the picture at the same time? Who the hell knows?*

Charley distracted me momentarily but I had a

mission to accomplish, so I walked into the psychiatrist's office. A secretary looked at me like I was from Mars.

"Yes," she said icily.

"Hi, I am a University student and I'd like to see Dr. Heatly," I said.

"Do you have an appointment? I don't have anyone down for an appointment today," she said.

"No, sorry. Could I make one?"

Two days later I was sitting in front of a middle-aged gentleman in a poorly fitting blue suit. He reminded me of Rotarians I had seen gathering at Furr's cafeteria in Odessa. White shirt. Thin gray tie. None of it fit and he didn't seem to match my image of a distinguished psychiatrist. Nevertheless, he was the adult on the other side of the desk and he had the Dr. before his name, so I attempted to convey my story to him. I told him about Janell's encounters with the Mystery Man, the magazines, and our fears. He seemed only to be half-listening and he was definitely impatient.

"Are you a UT student?" he asked.

"Yes, I am in my last class before graduating." I said.

"The young man? Is he?" he asked.

"I don't know. I assume he is or was," I responded.

"What's his name?'

"I told you that I don't know his name," I said.

"How can I help him then?" he asked.

"I don't know, but perhaps you could go to the house or…"

"No, students come to me; I don't go to them," he said.

"Well, OK, maybe, I can find out his name for you."

"OK, then maybe we can have him come in – if he is a current UT student," the doctor said.

"Good," I said, "and what reason would you give for bringing him in?" I asked.

"Well, because you wanted me to see him. What do you mean?" the doctor said.

To me it was obvious that the Mystery Man was a potential danger to my wife and me, and for this guy not to see that made no sense to me. He could not tell the kid that Janell and Shelly Williams, the couple running the apartments next door to the house he was illegally occupying, wanted the University Mental Health Services to call you in to talk about your penchant for hacking up girls' torsos on paper. There was just an outside chance that the Mystery Man would be miffed at being drawn away from his daily routine and perhaps just drop by Ye Ole Villa Rose Apartments to vent his fury on one or both of its managers.

"Can't you make up some reason for bringing him in here? You can't tell him I requested it," I said.

"What? What are you talking about? Look, you don't even know he's a UT student. Find out if he is and then we'll go from there," he said.

I knew walking out of there that I would not be coming back to the doctor's office. That was a bad idea. *Even if he brought the guy in,* I thought, *there was half a chance that a fifteen-minute talk with the doc might just push Mystery Man right over whatever edge he was perched on.* I resolved that minute not to come back to that office even if I found out the Mystery Man's name and even if he were a current UT student. No way.

Half-way home it also occurred to me to wonder: Why had Charley Fingernails been outside the Dr.'s office?

Chapter XII

Lollipop

Parts of the last days of July were dedicated to getting ready for the long drive to Washington, DC coming up mid-way through August. We wanted to stay in Austin as long as possible to squeeze out a few more dollars from Janell's job as a secretary in the Education Department and from my night watchman's job. Nevertheless, we had to get ready for the journey. Later in our lives – in fact every move after that one – preparing for a trip meant extensive packing of clothes, dishes, and books. Usually it would involve movers, boxes, and agonizing decisions of what to keep and what to throw away. Since we essentially owned nothing in 1966, getting ready for this particular adventure simply meant buying reading material for the long drive. That in turn meant a stop at the University Book Store on the Drag where I could buy *Current Theories of International Relations* and Janell could buy *Crime and Punishment* (since *Inside the Mind of a Serial Killer* would not be published until twenty years later).

"Hey, Lollipop," came a disembodied voice from behind the economics textbooks. Only one person on earth calls me that.

Linda Milburn is a redheaded beauty from Odessa, Texas. In junior high she and I performed a skit along with another couple. In it we jitterbugged to the pop tune *Lollipop, Lollipop* on stage in front of the school assembly. We had letters on our backsides and when the song ended, we turned to the audience to spell out POOH. Unfortunately our candidate for the 9th grade Presidency was named Hooper, so we had the letters backwards. He won anyway and Linda and I forged an even closer friendship. I was already pretty much taken with her, but Milburn, as we called her, and I only "went together" for two weeks of that 9th grade year. From then on we were friends, not lovers.

That friendship was deep. We went to the same school from junior high through college. We shared the same birthday, July 13, 1944, but somehow she reports being born on Friday while I was born on a Thursday. Her father, a state Judge, taught me how to tie a tie. Her boyfriends were close friends and usually fellow athletes. She was a Pepette, a kind of "spirit group" that assisted the Permian Panther cheerleaders in whipping the student body into frenzy for the football team. I was a football player. Despite all that shared history, we had seen each other only once in our mutual four years at UT. Not only that, I was not especially glad to see her that afternoon in the bookstore.

I left Odessa in 1962 unhappy with my world. My cousin Betty's death in 1961 soured me on Odessa and its rigid social structures. This was a place where my friends freely used the word "nigger" (though not Linda as far as I could remember). Many of them stayed stuck in high school and the conceptions of who was "popular" and who was not. Moreover, several visited me at UT only to pronounce me a communist for my support of civil rights and my opposition to Barry Goldwater and the war in Viet Nam. Now, Linda never did any of this, but she was from there. There was one other little problem. Late in the spring of my senior year of high school, Janell and I broke up for a short while. During that time, Linda, Jack Littlefield, Faith Ann Panowich, and I took a road trip to Austin to find places to live during our upcoming freshman year. Sometime just passed San Angelo, I yielded the driver's seat to Jack and climbed into the back seat with Linda. We made out off and on most of the rest of the way to Austin. She was the last girl I was "with" before Janell and I got back together, and I didn't want my wife of two years to be reminded of that – not now, for God's sake.

"Hey, Lollipop! Hey, Shell!" she repeated. "How's the hell are you?" Linda was a bit of Auntie Mame with a lot of Molly Brown thrown in.

"Oh, hi Linda, fine," I said. I was obligated to add: "How are you?"

Linda and Janell hugged - Sorority girl meets

proto-married-Hippie-revolutionary. Janell adored Linda, and still does.

"Hey, you, have you already graduated?" Not waiting for an answer, she said: "Seems like I haven't seen you since I lost my virginity in the backseat of your Daddy's pink Cadillac."

Janell laughed and I turned the color of Linda's hair.

"Linda! You know we didn't do it," I protested. We were standing in the middle of an aisle of UT's largest bookstore. Dozens of people milled about. I admit I was torn between two emotions: set the record straight or take credit for having sex with easily one of the two or three prettiest women I had ever known. With Janell standing there, it seemed prudent to emphasize the reality of my complete failure ever to get laid in high school.

"Maybe you didn't Lollipop, but I sure did!"

God save me from gorgeous West Texas women with tart tongues, but then maybe Janell could use a reminder that I, too, might be of some interest to the opposite sex.

I laughed awkwardly at Linda's declaration but didn't - couldn't - respond. Janell laughed, hugged Linda, and deftly attempted to excuse us on the grounds that we were in the final stages of getting ready to move to Washington, DC. Linda flashed a look saying "why would you ever move to that place?" but she didn't say a word. Instead she ignored it and launched into a West Texas story since almost all West Texans are story-tellers by nature.

"Guess who I saw in Odessa last weekend? Roland Gladden! He was your runnin' buddy, wasn't he Shell? I'll never forget you two. He'd piss off a teacher and you'd get in trouble. He'd steal your motor scooter and you'd get the ticket. He'd get the Student Council store opened up before school and you'd end up working the extra hours! What a riot!"

She was right. What Roland lacked in brains and charm, he made up for in sheer luck. I bailed him out of many a jam and saved him in many a class, but we had fun every step of the way. We stayed friends regardless of the torture and trouble the relationship always meant. The memory made me smile.

"You ever see him, Shell?" she asked.

"No, not really," I replied. "We don't go out much when we go home." How could Linda know how I felt about Odessa, the meaninglessness of high school and football nowadays? Why should it come up?

"Oh, well, have fun in Dog City when you get there. Y'all come see me when you get back to Odessa," Linda said. Someone else, a "hairdo," as I called them, distracted Linda and as quickly as she reentered my life, she disappeared again. When would we see ever again? Four years? Twenty Years? Never?

"Linda Milburn," I said. "What a trip."

"Yeah," she replied, "I have always liked her." She was not upset by the Cadillac story and she did not seem jealous. She didn't seem anything, except perhaps a little wistful.

""You know, I miss that guy," she said finally as we rounded the corner where they kept the classic novels.

Guy? Linda? No, Roland, I thought. "I thought you barely knew Roland Gladden," I said.

"No," she said, "not that guy - the guy who used to be so funny, so happy, and so popular in high school. The guy you used to be."

CHAPTER XIII

MUSTANG

The hammering began late one July night. I heard it instantly, but Janell initially had to strain to hear it. Unmistakably it came from the old house next door, and it emanated from the upper floors, not the lower.

"He's building something," Janell speculated. We slid open the window; moved to the other twin bed next to it; and sat peering into the Texas night to see if there were a light flickering from the upper reaches of the house. We could see none, but the sound was distinctive and it was incessant. We sat there and listened for maybe five minutes or so.

"Yeah, I guess, he's not fixing anything," I said eventually.

"Maybe he's booby trapping the house for ..."

"You," I said, seriously.

"Will you please lighten up?" she responded. "I don't know what he's doing, but I am certain he doesn't know I am watching him. That one incident went too fast. He barely saw me. Besides, we are almost out of here. A little over two weeks and we will be in Washington, DC."

More silence followed. She sat inside of me leaning her chin on the windowsill staring into the darkness. I moved close and fit my body close to hers and placed my arms around her. When we lay in our bed, we called this "scuddling." Here we were half sitting, half lying on the bed. Neither of us was quite aware when the hammering stopped. By then we had incorporated the rhythmic sound into our thoughts and I tried to remember the last time I had paid attention to the Texas sky. Had it been my senior year in high school when my gang of friends slept at the Monahans Sand hills? That was four years prior and a lifetime ago. Running into Linda Milburn had made me think of the fun times I had in West Texas, but that moment looking at that sky made me recall what West Texas sometimes felt like. Curious timing too – just as we were about to leave Texas forever. Sleep came easily.

"The doctor didn't work," Janell said the next morning. "We have to call the police," Janell said.

"I agree," I said. That would be the responsible thing and this hammering cannot be good. How long did it last?"

"Last night it stopped before you started snoring," she said, "but he started up again before 6:00 AM this morning."

"So I slept through it, huh? Guess my night watchman skills are pretty well honed to the finest international standards."

"Yeah, right" she said, "There's not a birth certificate safe in the entire state."

"You call the police," I said. "I did the doctor. Besides I promised my dad I'd drop by the car wash this afternoon. He said he had a surprise for me."

"OK, sure," she said.

It was a surprise. My father had never valued my college education. Indeed he kicked me out of the house and refused to pay for UT when he found out I was going away to school. He wanted me to stay in Odessa, attend the local junior college, and then go to car wash management school. He tried everything from yelling at me to faking a heart attack to kicking me out of the house to keep me from going. He never knew my grades; he had no idea I graduated Phi Beta Kappa; and he could not fathom why after graduating UT I would now go on for more education.

"Hell, you're gonna have to earn a living sometime," he would inevitably say.

"Well, you could always pay me for the years I worked at the car wash between ages eight an eighteen and then maybe I could afford more school," I would inevitably respond.

Today was not like that. He and Dee were not defensive and they did not try to cajole me to ask Janell to come out to their place for dinner. When I drove into the car wash parking lot, the two of them were already standing there next to his new Pontiac.

"Get in the car, Shelly Bill. Let's go for a drive," he said.

That was typical. I was to do something for which there was no explanation. There would, of course, be no inquiries about how much time I had to devote to such a drive. He would not wonder if Janell might need my presence at home. I was to do as he instructed. I gave half a thought to declining or making up a lie about when I should get back home, but instead I just got his car and went along. It might have been the unusually friendly smile Dee had on her face when Daddy said to get in the car. It might have been that I really didn't have a book to read, a paper to write or madman to apprehend. And I didn't go to work that night until 11:00 PM either. So I went.

Daddy drove to the northern edge of Austin to a huge car lot. It was some kind of Ford dealership.

"Ford's got a new car out, Son. It's called a Mustang. I want you to pick one out."

"I can't afford a car. I don't want a Mustang. I like the Fairlane." My negative responses were programmed, as automatic as a Swiss watch.

"No," Shelly," Dee said. "Take a look. Your Daddy wants to give you a graduation gift."

This is the guy who never accepted a gift I ever gave him in his life. This is the guy who came home drunk late on Christmas Eve and brought unwrapped expensive toys with the price tags still dangling from them. This is the guy who bought my fiancée a pair of shorty pajamas for Christmas and asked her to model them for him. This the guy who…

God, that Mustang was a fine-looking car.

Chapter XIV

Sprezzatura

Mixed emotions were the order of the day. We had a new car, a red one, but Janell and I wanted a blue one. My German class was over and I made an A, but the usual doubts about my abilities flooded my mind as I contemplated graduate school. It was exciting to think about moving to Washington, but Janell and I calculated that we might even have to double the $65 a month we were paying for rent in order to live there. Could she continue school? The hammering from the house continued, but we had not seen the Mystery Man again and there had been no more thefts or Peeping Tom incidents. Best of all, Janell discerned that I was anxious about Don, so she just openly told me that they had not had sex. But now I had a far more illusive competitor for her affections – the relaxed and happy person I used to be. We had both studied under a master teacher at UT, Dr. Benjamin Harrison, in the English Department. He explained an Italian Renaissance concept to us called sprezzatura. The term didn't quite mean grace under pressure. It meant doing brave, amazing, or artful things with seeming indifference or casual disregard. Seems like I once had it, but stress, self-doubt, and worry had eroded much of it. Now where did I last put it?

Janell had real difficulty getting the Austin police to come to our apartment to find out about the Mystery Man. We could not go to them during the day because she needed to work every minute of every day. She had no leave time. They twice scheduled to come to our apartment, but no one ever showed up. She got a detective's name, Kevin Cooper, but they played telephone tag all day. Finally on a Friday night, July 29, Cooper and another detective showed up at our apartment literally as we were about to go out to the first movie we had seen in months, a happy little ditty called Who's Afraid of Virginia Wolf? It was part of my "get out and live a little" plan. Not tonight, however, not tonight.

The detectives initially seemed more interested in us, especially Janell, than they did in our situation. In addition to our names, what our positions were in the apartment complex, who owned the Rose, where else we worked, and what we had seen, they seemed awfully chatty about Texas football and what movie we wanted to see. I pressed them to the "case," but in the end they seemed to think that we had no case. Janell recounted the petty thefts and the harrowing visit to the house. She didn't mention the hammering since last we checked hammering was not illegal. Cooper occasionally wrote something down. The other guy never took his eyes off Janell and never said a word. She finished her story and waited for a response.

"That's it? Anything else?" Cooper asked.

"Like what?" Janell asked back.

"Well, did he hurt you, threaten you, steal anything from you?"

"No, but he stole from our tenants," she said.

"Oh? Which tenants? Do they wish to file a complaint?"

"No, I mean, I guess not, but what about the pictures of those women up in his attic?" Janell asked.

"That's weird, but not illegal," Cooper pointed out.

"The house," I interjected, "he's illegally occupying the house."

"Oh?" Cooper said. "Do you own the property? Do you know who does?"

Janell knew that these guys weren't going to do a thing. She asked the obvious question: "You can't do anything until a crime is committed, right? And you don't consider squatting worth your time to worry about?"

"Looks like you kids may be spooked by this guy, but he seems harmless to us. No offense, but I think you have it about right."

"You kids." It's true. We were 22 and 20 at the time. It never occurred to us that the police would consider our call a nuisance. They asked those questions in part because they doubted we even managed the Rose. They were used to homicides, domestic disputes, robberies, and the like. We were simply kids, UT students of no social standing, distracting them from their real work. We had made the Mystery Man into some sort of fantasy project that kept us busy in the summer but was of no real concern to a serious adult. Bummer.

Janell thought otherwise.

"Mr. Cooper, you're making a big mistake," she said. "This young man is troubled. He is in the early stages of some kind on psychological melt down that may end in tragedy. Most of all he needs help, and we are at our wits' end on what to do about it. If you can't do anything, what would you suggest we do?"

"You may be right, Mrs. Williams," he said "but without a crime or without a complaint from the owner of that house, there's nothing we can do. And there's nothing you can do either," he added. "Just for your own protection, I strongly advise against going back into that house. In truth, you are trespassing."

The detectives left after about an hour, but we did not feel like going to the movies after that. We felt empty. I wondered if we had gotten sucked up into our own little drama, but I was proud of Janell's clear and well-reasoned defense of our concerns.

The summer had taken a turn over the past few weeks. The well-ordered life we had known as students had given way to luxurious afternoons with friends and TV in the early weeks but those had in turned into heavy, pointless, disconcerting days and nights of waiting and suspended animation. As we killed time preparing to leave Austin every day grew hotter than the next. Perhaps the heat had gotten to us. There might really be no mystery to solve, but a kid's life seemed to be spinning out of control. That very day I saw Charley Fingernails driving down 19th street with a pretty blonde. His wife? Why does he keep popping up or am I just more aware of him since this all began? All of it seemed so anticipatory, more like a prelude than an ending or a departure. Still nothing actually occurred. It just seemed about to occur, but what? When?

"I'll tell you what, Honey," I said. "Let's not try to see Virginia Wolf tonight. Let's get in that new car and drive over past the river to Hill's Café. I intend to ply you with sizzling steak, take you on a ride out by the lake, find a place to dance, and then rent a motel room. What happens next I promise never to tell."

She knew that only the drive part of that scenario could happen. We had no money. She also knew that inside I was a jumble about school, the Mystery Man, Charley, and money. She appreciated that I chose to ignore it all and offer her a glorious night on the town. Whatever happened next could not bother me that night. Come what may.

West Texas sprezzatura.

Chapter XV

Scholz's

In 1966 Scholz's Beer Garden was Austin politicos' favorite haunt. Lyndon Johnson's protégé (and that means the President's protégé), Ben Barnes, a thirty-three year old wunderkind, was there at least once a week. Everyone from paid political consultants (a fairly new phenomenon in 66) to sitting legislators to state bureaucrats turned up at Scholz's to drink draft beer, tell lies, and flirt with the young waitresses. Only UT students outnumbered the politicians and the wannabe politicians.

On summer nights the long tables, the short stools, and the tiny bathrooms were overflowing. The inside dining room filled up as well, but only after the huge crowds occupied every available inch of the table space underneath the ivy-encrusted lattice rope covering the backyard beer garden. To most people Scholz's was heaven-on-earth—cold beer, endless political conversation, and good looking women. What could be better?

I officially hated Scholz's. I didn't drink; state politics bored me; and Janell was my woman. Besides, a couple of years back I briefly entered the world that these guys represented and the experience soured me on the whole lot.

It was 1964, in the fall, and the presidential election was barely six weeks away. I had joined the UT Young Democrats, though I went to just one meeting. But one Thursday night at a LBJ rally, I found myself face-to-face with the President of the United States. He shook my hand on his way to the podium and from that podium he talked about the Great Society, the end of racism, defense of Social Security, and realism and restraint in foreign affairs. I was hooked, and for the next few weeks I became omnipresent at the LBJ Headquarters on Congress Ave. in downtown Austin. I made phone calls; fetched coffee; and passed out bumper stickers. I believed. Barry Goldwater scared me and I thought the TV ad with the little girl with the mushroom cloud looming behind her was a completely objective depiction of the potential dangers of a Goldwater presidency.

Then one night I found myself at the Headquarters much later than usual. In fact, I was the only volunteer on the floor and only the "suits" were left in the front office. I didn't know their names and they didn't know mine, but one of them called to me anyway.

"Hey, Kid. Wanna drink?"

I walked in the room even though I didn't drink. I wanted to know what these guys might say about "politics in our time" or about the issues of the day. Around the office they had such an air of confidence and a grasp of political minutia that bespoke of long-ago campaigns and life and death struggles. I wanted a close-up glimpse into that world of experience.

They were cool in the old "His Girl Friday" kind of cool. All were coatless and hatless, and they wore white shirts with thin black ties. They were the pros and, true to my expectations, they had one-half a fifth of Three Roses Whiskey sitting on the coffee table in front of them. Stolen hotel glasses with a little to a lot of whiskey also sat there. Not one of them had ice. The banter came quickly and easily as they discussed not the presidential race but the battle for the Senate. How would "Ralph" (liberal Senator Ralph Yarborough) do in Grayson and Collin counties in North Texas against that rich Yankee George Bush? Lyndon would pull Ralph through, but it'd be closer than '58, etc. Dallas attitudes were moving north but not enough to break Democratic dominance in the area.

Transfixed, I said nothing.

After ten minutes, however, the conversation heated up as the rest of the Three Roses disappeared.

"That fucking Connally (then Governor of Texas) is doing nothing to help the Party along."

"He might as well be a Republican."

"And Lyndon just smiles and kisses his ass."

"Kennedy thought he could come to Texas and get those assholes to get with the plan."

"Connally's just waitin' to screw us over. You'll see."

"As far as I'm concerned, Oswald shot the wrong sunavbitch. I wish he had hit Connally in the head and not Jack."

For the second time in my life, I left a function via the backdoor. Wandering home in a daze, I pondered the distinction between liberal and conservative Democrats. I knew they were at odds, but, in my youthful naiveté, I had no idea what would cause one faction to wish death for the other. It was not the last time I heard someone from "my side" wish harm for the other, but every time it happens, I consider outrange the only appropriate response. Later when Connally actually switched to the Republicans and served, of all people, Richard Nixon, the only pleasure I got from his defection was that some of the guys in the room must have blown a gasket.

When I walked into Scholz's that July night two years later, all I could see was wall-to-wall politicians. Why had I come? Tony, Mary Ann, Janell and I simply wanted to be able to say that we had been to the famous Scholz's while we were at UT. Besides, I had a plan to "live a little" and take my mind off of Austin policemen, psychiatrists, and lost boys. The atmosphere wasn't all that bad if you forgot you were surrounded by former insurance men turned legislators. It was loud, colorful, and relaxed. Janell and Mary Ann broke out in smiles while Tony looked like he had taken a drink of spoiled milk. At first I shared Tony's reaction, but then I heard...the band.

I had no idea Scholz's had music and maybe on most nights they didn't. Tonight they did. Situated in the far back corner of the garden, there was a blues band, a white one, but nevertheless a blues band. I was transported back to Odessa as a teenager when I went to the "other side of the tracks" with the black guys who worked for my dad's car wash. Sipping on red soda pop and munching on barbeque chicken, I got to watch "the boys" and their ladies get down. And now at Scholz's, as white as these musicians were, they were playing Ray Charles, BB King, and Fats Domino. Tony may have wanted to discuss Che Guevarra or Dole Fruit's misdeeds in Hawaii and Central America, but I wanted to dance.

But no one else was dancing. Mary Ann said what a lot of people were probably thinking.

"These white folks couldn't dance if they wanted to."

Janell smiled. "Well, a couple of them could."

"Oh yeah!," Mary Ann issued a challenge, "Just who?"

"We grew up on this stuff, right, Shelly?"

Our best friends had no idea. Tony took note.

"Go ahead, my man. We will if you will." World revolution could wait. This could be as entertaining as three hotels on Park Place.

Janell and I did not hesitate. After all, our first kiss came after we skipped school assembly to twist in the backroom of the School Store. Chubby Checker did his "thang" and then I did mine. Dancing had always been our little secret. Janell could move to the groove and eyes turned her way instantly. How could they not?

Countless hours on the south side of Odessa also prepared me. The effortless and sensual abandon of my black friends there was an awakening for me and I had almost forgotten it. But Freddie Mae Jackson, one of my dad's faithful workers, never let me just watch. She took the lead in showing me how. And she did not patronize the white boy or assume I had no rhythm.

"Shelly Bill, forget the steps. Stop watchin' they feet and just let the music make you move. Ain't nobody gonna laugh at you. Just find the beat and go wit it."

It didn't look good when I first tried, but she was right. Nobody laughed. On the contrary, women said things like "Rock on, lil man." "Oh, yeah, baby." The guys smiled and offered me drinks of hooch. Yes, I was the boss's son, but he wasn't there, and it got better and better. "The Mashed Potato," "The Twist," and just plain ole Boogie Woogie—I learned them all, and that night at Scholz's I found them again. The band loved it. Tony and Mary Ann had their own thing workin'. Janell and I made love on the dance floor.

Was Freddie Mae offering me a key to understanding my own sprezzatura? To find it, maybe all I had to do was "go wit it." That magical night at Scholz's, it certainly worked for us.

Chapter XVI

Busted II

Janell was not giving up on her own detective work. She was Nancy Drew in hip huggers. The psychiatrist and the cops were of no use, but she was determined at least to find out the Mystery Man's name and his background. Was no one to care about this guy? Would no one take responsibility before something untoward occurred? She would. She had to. She had one day to do it though, a Saturday, because her sister, Tira, was coming on Sunday to spend a week with us. Janell would not allow anything to interfere with showing her little sister a good time in Austin. The truth is that Janell felt guilty about getting married at eighteen and leaving home with a younger sister and an infant brother left in a household where her father was disabled and her mom had a fairly low paying clerical job. Tira and Brad, her one-year-old surprise brother, were everything to her, and Janell's "getting out" of West Texas always meant conversely a sort of abandonment of her precious siblings. It was always all the more galling over time since neither of them ever saw any rationale for getting out themselves. West Texas was fine with them. In any event Saturday was the only day Janell had to peruse recent UT yearbooks to see if the Mystery Man's face appeared in one of them. She just needed a name, a hometown, or something. I dropped her off on the Drag just a half block from the Undergraduate Library where no doubt she could find a yearbook section.

Somehow I doubted the Mystery Man, even if he had attended UT, had posed for a yearbook picture. I tried to remember if I had ever done so. Maybe my freshman year, but never after. That was just another sign that I had changed dramatically since coming to UT. In a school where social status ruled everything, I cared for none of it. The Greek system that dominated UT social life offended me totally. As a freshman, a group called the Kappa Alphas "rushed" me. I had no idea who the KAs were or what they stood for, but I had been in social clubs in high school so I attended one of their functions before classes began. Some older UT guy from Odessa I barely knew sought me out after reading an article about me in the local newspaper, the Odessa American. He invited me to come to a KA party. The KAs, it seems, were dedicated to keeping the Confederacy alive. In the frat house where I attended a dinner, the confederate flag was everywhere and there were multitudes of pictures of the "Old South Ball" hanging on the walls. At the dinner table we were served exclusively by black men wearing tails and many, if not most, of the rich white boys at the table talked openly about the "boys" or "niggers" waiting on them. I made it through the salad serving before I simply got up, walked out the sliding glass door leading to the backyard, walked across the yard, scaled the brick fence, and got the hell out of there. From that day on, unfairly or not, all fraternities at UT stood for racism and snobbery in my mind. I never even considered joining another.

Had I gone too far in my rejection of social niceties? Not being a KA did not mean I should become a hermit. Making the grades I needed for graduate school and fighting war and oppression, I told myself, should be my only focus as an undergraduate. Now the problem seemed to be that I had lost myself in all of that studying, protesting, and judging. While not necessarily a tragedy for me, it had cost Janell more than I realized. What had I thought about marriage? A wife would love me no matter what — like a parent. Whether I am good or bad, happy or sad, the love would always be there. She'd care for me and forgive and understand my moods.

Janell would have none of it. OK, she said, I understand the pressure you are under and the Gulf of Tonkin was a sham, but there are two people in this house and neither one of us has the right to inflict doom or depression on the other. Sure, I love you, but get over yourself and be aware that you have to work at this relationship. Well, she didn't say it exactly like that, but that is what it meant. She did say this: "When we have a child, will you let yourself be happy so the kid will can be happy as well?" That hurt and it hit home.

My father never bothered with the atmosphere he created in our household. That Saturday morning, that very day, I decided that my fear of "bad things" would not invade our home again and I would try to rediscover the guy who was voted "wittiest" his junior year and then "friendliest" his senior year of high school. It's not always been easy, but it's been the right thing to do. I went for another drive around Austin that afternoon in my bright red Mustang. It wasn't a convertible, but it felt like one. I felt like a new man.

Janell meanwhile combed the *Cactus*, the UT yearbook. She looked at the 1966, 1965, and 1964 volumes. The Mystery Man looked so young, she didn't think it possible that he had come before then. She could find no picture of him or perhaps she could not recognize who he used to be. There was also still the fleeting possibility that the guy had never been a student at UT. She tried one more thing. She walked back to our neighborhood and started knocking on doors. Perhaps someone had seen him since she last inquired. Perhaps someone had actually met him, had a conversation with him, given him advice, or told him to move on. Perhaps she could call the realty company advertising the house for sale to find out if there had been a complaint about him. Perhaps the house's owners knew something. Late in the afternoon, the sheer absence of anything tangible frustrated her. No one had seen him. No one had heard him. No one knew anything. She thought briefly about going into the house pretending to be a prospective buyer. She even went past the house. She stopped, turned and went through the front gate. She decided, however, that wasn't a good idea, so she retreated back to the sidewalk. What a day, she thought, as she walked the short distance from the Victorian house to the edge of the Rose's parking lot. *All this and I haven't gotten anything. I haven't even seen him in weeks.*

What she didn't know is at that very moment he could see her.

Shelly's freshman picture

CHAPTER XVII

MONDAY, MONDAY

"The thing I like about Austin is that something's always happening," said Janell's little sister, Tira.

We were sitting at the stop light at the intersection of Guadalupe, the Drag, and 24th Street. The Varsity Theater was to our right. The principal buildings of the UT campus lay across the street and to our left. A row of stores -- jewelry, clothing and most importantly bookstores -- lay ahead of us and to the right. It was a hot, sunny day, not an unusual August 1st in Austin, Texas, but there were lots of people around that day despite the heat. Pedestrians, drivers, shoppers, and people just milling about were everywhere. It was approaching noon and Tira and I were on the way to pick up Janell for a quick lunch. She was to meet us in the Sutton Hall Driveway, just a step outside her office at the Educational Psychology Office. We were three minutes away and it was three minutes to 12:00 noon.

We saw nothing out of the ordinary. We were aware

of nothing unusual. We had the radio up high and I will swear until the day I die we were listening to the Mamas and Papas' "Monday, Monday" that Monday. We drove the half block from 24th to the stoplight in front of the University Co-op Book Store in just a minute or two. I was fully engaged in making Tira feel welcome to Austin and frankly in showing off the UT campus. All the previous night we had talked about almost nothing except the Mystery Man and the absurdity of the Austin Police and the UT psychiatrist. Tira was thirteen at the time, and she was prone to even more lurid imaginings of the Mystery Man's actions than we were. For the first time ever, the events of the summer had become a "story," and while it didn't seem real in the brilliance of the noonday sun, it gave us a lively topic to discuss. At this point, however, the Mystery Man was not on our minds. The sun, the music, the low growling of empty stomachs, and the Austin spectacle around us captured our attention. We were quite satisfied just to look.

Just as we pulled up to the light in front of the Co-op, I heard loud and frequent gunshots. I knew it was gunshots. I am from West Texas and have been around rifles and shotguns my whole life. I looked to my left and saw a black man ducking behind a low retaining wall at the west entrance to the UT Mall. I rolled down my window and yelled out to him: "Where's it coming from?"

He crouched down behind the wall, pointed over his head and up, and yelled back: "The Tower."

People to my left and right scattered to find cover. The loud gunshots made it sound like the gunman or gunmen were much closer than the Tower. It was half a block away on campus and 307 feet in the air, but I didn't doubt the man's answer. I was unaware but just minutes before a paperboy on a bike had been gunned down just a few feet from where I stopped. A crowd had gathered around him but it had dissipated in a panic by the time Tira and I arrived at the spot. I saw no bodies and no blood, but I didn't need to. I reacted immediately to the fact that we were caught in the line of fire of a gunman. After the ordeal was over, I heard that many people believed that two or more people had been on the Tower shooting at pedestrians on and around the UT campus. My initial thoughts were one gunman, one long-range rifle, and one desire to kill as many people as possible. This was the sort of "bad thing" I anticipated.

Seconds after the man told me that there was gunfire from the Tower, I slammed the Mustang into reverse and drove backwards down the Drag on the opposite side of the street. Thus, I was speeding backwards toward 24th Street. Tira was not screaming, but she was not calm either. I didn't say that someone was shooting but my actions told her that we were escaping from imminent danger. Going forty miles an hour backwards not always in a perfect straight line was frightening enough. My great fear, however, was that a bright red car racing backwards down the Drag would draw the sniper's attention. Actually I soon realized that I was OK for the block back to 24th Street because trees and buildings interfered with the sniper's line of vision. Turning left at that corner going in reverse might call attention to us, however. I did it anyway because I knew I had to get out at that intersection to warn people not to approach the University campus.

I took the corner and intentionally blocked the way of a couple of cars coming to the intersection. I backed the Mustang up and them too. I pulled the car up on the curb, part of the way up on the sidewalk. I made sure that Tira stayed in the car and down, even though parked that way, she was out of the shooter's line of sight. Then I did something I knew I had to do. I stood out in the middle of 24th Street and waived drivers and pedestrians away from the Drag.

Waving my hands, I said: "Go Back! Somebody's shooting from the Tower!"

One guy rolled down his window, stared at me incredulously, listened to the loud retorts of the far away weapon, and said: "That's a shotgun. It can't reach here."

I said: "You don't know it's a shotgun. It sounds too loud for one to me."

The woman in his car said: "Let's go back, Honey. Don't take a chance." Macho Man huffed and puffed but he put it in reverse.

I continued to direct traffic at the corner of 24th and Guadalupe for a few minutes. I could tell that the shooter was firing the other way, at least temporarily. I cannot be sure how many people left that area because I warned them, but it may have been a dozen or so. The shots grew much louder, however, and glancing back at the car, I could see that Tira's head was bobbing up and that she was clearly worried. And she was alone. For the first time another thought struck me. Janell? Was she on the Drag waiting for us? Had she been hit? Why in God's name had I not thought of her first? I slowly walked back to the Mustang where Tira was getting more upset by the minute.

"What say we go down the street and call your sister?" I said almost casually.

"Will she be OK?" Tira asked anxiously.

"I'll bet she's OK," I said. "Girls from West Texas know their way around guns." I lied. I had no idea whether or not Janell would be safe. I had only one thing going for me. In the history of our marriage, before and since, she has never been on time for anything. She was never outside waiting for me at 12:00 PM when I came for her. I was always there on time or a little earlier. This pattern has not varied for forty years. I prayed that she had been true to form that day and had not broken her pattern to meet her kid sister.

I got in the Mustang and sped around the corner away from the University on the Drag. I drove a couple of blocks down, surely far enough away from the Tower to avoid the shots, and we dashed into a small Hemphill's Book Store at about 26th and Guadalupe. The clerk was standing behind the counter watching the Tower from the small plate glass window in the store. We walked in and I asked: "Mind if I use the phone to call my wife? She's working on campus."

The clerk turned white at first, but she, too, wanted to avoid scaring the teenager with me. "Oh, sure," she said as she slid the phone over to me.

Please, God, let her answer. She did at the first ring.

"Are you all right?" we asked simultaneously.

"Is Tira OK?" she blurted. I let them talk and for the first time I heard myself described as a hero. Tira rapidly told Janell how quickly I had reacted, how skillfully I had driven, and how bravely I had directed traffic with gunfire all around. Janell was none too happy to hear about any of that and as soon as I got back on the phone, she gave me a simple command: "Get that child back home now!" Shortly after we drove away from Hemphill's, a man a little farther down the street came out of a barbershop to see what was going on and the sniper dropped him with a single bullet. The shooter's range was incredible and by my best recollection, had he seen me or had he chosen to aim at me, I was in his line of sight for no less than twenty minutes. Later we learned that seven people were shot and two or three died at the corner of 24th and Guadalupe. I was upset that I had not been there to tell them to leave the area.

Tira and I drove home. We in fact watched the rest of the gruesome events live on Austin TV. It lasted for an hour-and-twenty minutes. I called my parents and Janell's during that time to assure them that we were safe. The lines were jammed and it took awhile, but I got through. Then we heard that the Austin Police had killed a young man at the top of the Tower. It was over and the Tower sniper was dead.

I left Tira with some friends I went back to the University. As I left the Rose's parking lot, I glanced down the street.

"Was it you, Mystery Man, was it you?"

CHAPTER XVIII

AFTERMATH

In my four years at the University of Texas, I rarely felt like I was part of any sort of community. I went in and out of huge classes and I walked across the Mall just like everyone else. I ate at the Student Union and I studied at the Undergraduate Academic Center with throngs of other students. But I was not ever part of anything. Only twice did I have a sense of being connected to the people around me. The first time was during the Cuban Missile Crisis my freshman year and the second was that day, August 1, 1966. When I got back to campus, people were still in shock but they had come out of their offices and various hiding places just to be with other human beings. We milled around the blood-streaked spots on the South Mall where two dozen or so were killed or wounded. We congregated at the base of the Tower as a hospital gurney brought out "the guy," the shooter. We looked, but we could not see. He was covered, so we could not determine if he were the Mystery Man, "our guy."

Janell had been saved from the on campus carnage

by what she calls her "work fugue," the fog-like state she often enters when absorbed with a problem. She sat at her desk contemplating files and records, so she was not in harm's way when the shooting began. Friends and colleagues of hers wandered out to the Mall to see "where the shots were coming from" or to see the "shoot out" occurring there. She was anxious to walk around the campus to find out if they were OK. Besides, all of us were in a state of semi-shell shock and we could not tear ourselves away the scene. We went to be together.

Newspaper accounts and at least one book have cataloged the dead and injured from this rampage. Eventually seventeen died and forty-two were injured. A wife, a mother, a paperboy, brilliant students, revered faculty, someone's sister, another's son. The shooter himself would die and his death would spark controversy about which of the two brave men, Houston McCoy or Ramiro Martinez, who confronted him actually fired the fatal shot or shots. The Tower Sniper's motives and the reasons for the event have been analyzed ad nauseam. Did the tumor they eventually found in his brain contribute to his mental illness? Did he hate his father so much that he wanted to embarrass him by committing such a heinous act? Similarly, did he kill his wife and his mother prior to taking to the Tower to avoid embarrassing them by his actions and to allow them to escape the horrors of life as quickly as possible? Why are serial killers so often white, middle class young men with tortured souls?

These questions would occupy the minds of those of us who were there, and millions who weren't, for decades to come, but that day all we could think of was survival. Why had we lived and others died? How close had we come to death in an instant? When the sniper's range and incredible accuracy were revealed, we lost our youthful sense of invulnerability while gaining an appreciation that any minute - any second actually - could be our last on earth. As dozens of us stood there, we marveled at the scene and we reached out to one another.

"Where were you when it started?"

"Did you know anyone who was hit?"

"So, there was only one guy? Who was he?"

"Who got him?"

When the chattering died down and at long last we walked away, not one of failed to glance at the Tower to see if a rifle barrel were edging out from the parapet. It would be forever thus.

Janell and I could only focus on the moment.

"Where is Tira? Is she OK?" asked the worried big sister.

"Mahmoud, the sweet boy from Kuwait, and his friend, Mohamed are with her,"

I said.

"Sure, of course, she loves Mahmoud," Janell responded.

"It's odd, you know," she said. "I heard someone say the sniper's name. It's another Charley. Charles

Whitman, they said."

"Oh my God," I replied. "That's it. That's his last name."

"Whose?" she asked.

"Charley Fingernails," I replied. "His last name is Whitman. I recall it now."

"The Marine?" she said.

"Yes, the former Marine," I responded.

The revelation that Charles Whitman was Charley Fingernails shook me up. I had said that I would not be surprised if he had a violent outburst, but this? Over the ensuing days and weeks we would hear more about Whitman. We would hear of his spotty academic and Marine Corps records and we would hear of his difficult relationship with his father and his reaction to his parents' divorce. All of this may have been the context for his decision to go to the Tower to kill people but they could not be the reasons. As a young person, I had to compare myself to him. He was embarrassed by his father's employment as a plumber and his father drove him hard to be a success in business. My Dad worked at a carwash and he drove me and on occasion humiliated me. Whitman was a list maker and compulsive about self-improvement. Those traits could be on my resume. He married young and struggled to make ends meet. He worshiped his mother and thought she had been wronged in the divorce. Ditto. The differences were his lack of academic success and his involvement with the Marine Corps. If my youthful liberal inclinations were to blame his love of hunting or his stint in the Corps for his the carnage he wrought that day, my walk across the campus disabused me of either of those prejudices very quickly.

What is often overlooked in accounts of the Whitman Tower shootings is the heroism of several young men (whose names may be lost forever) who ran across the Mall to try to bring the wounded to safety. We heard about them that day, walking away from the Tower. Some were Viet Nam veterans, we were told. They may have been former Marines. They may have loved guns and may have been expert riflemen. They may have been white; they may have had troubled relationships with their fathers; or they may have been struggling in school. Who knows? Subsequent accounts never mention the backgrounds, interests, or personalities of these heroes. As Janell and I strolled around campus, however, we met other students who could not believe what these guys had done. People lay on the hot concrete in various stages of dying and, had not these men rescued some of them, the body count of August 1 would have been much higher.

Similarly, few accounts ever note the heroism of the ambulance drivers who raced across the narrow interuniversity drive from the Drag across the southern face of the Tower to retrieve the wounded. Whitman shot at these vehicles just as he shot at the rest of us. Ironically the drivers had to come off strike to make these runs. They were protesting the City Council's refusal to raise their wages to astronomical figure of $1.25 an hour. They responded to the Whitman shootings immediately and they attempted to save lives by getting there as fast as they could. They didn't wait until it was over. I had also reacted quickly, but I didn't know the full extent of the risks. The men, vets and others, who tried to help and the ambulance drivers who retrieved the dead and wounded knew the risks full well and still reacted. Where are the books about them?

I vowed at that very moment to focus my memories of August 1, 1966 on the living and not the dead. That too was a survival instinct. The tragedy that day exceeded the slaughter of Richard Speck, of Ed Gein, of Charles Starkweather. Not until Timothy McVeigh, another disgruntled former soldier, killed 243 on April 19, 1995 did the nation ever witness a mass murder of such dimensions. It was too much for us to digest. Janell and I, of course, have no answers about why such events occur, but we also have made it a habit to find out how people can cope with such tragedies and not despair. Over our lifetime, we have been amazed by the stories we have heard. Leaving the campus that afternoon, however, we were bewildered, grateful, and even more troubled. Janell said it best:

"Charley and the Mystery Man have been linked all summer. What effect will all this have on him? Will there be a copycat reaction? You know, we can't just let this go."

I knew.

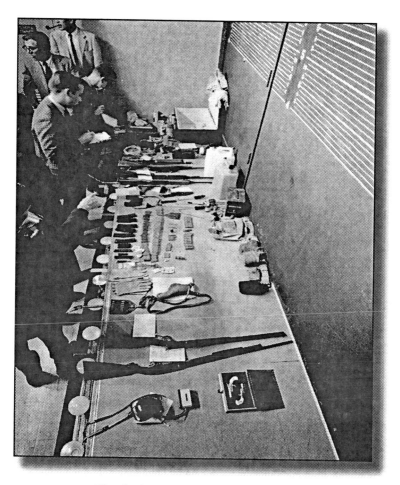

Charlie's arsenal, Shel Hershorn

CHAPTER XIX

SWEET DREAMS

Janell and I resolved "to do something" about the Mystery Man, but we had no idea what. That evening was the first night of our lives after the Tower. It was not easy to get through. It occurred to me not to go to work that night, but as the clock moved closer to 11:00 PM, the reality that I had to leave struck me. Prior to my leaving, we watched TV, listened to the radio, and talked with other Rose tenants out on the lawn. People still needed to communicate. It was necessary somehow to differentiate ourselves from Whitman, but it was troubling for some to think that a university student, not a common drifter or a closeted maniac, had done this incomprehensible thing. That part was not hard for me. I had experienced it before, in high school, when a "popular" boy had killed my cousin.

My mind wandered to the encounters Whitman and I had had. In particular I thought about the day I saw him outside of the psychiatrist's office. Had his demons driven him there? Had my presence stopped him from getting help? In subsequent days we would learn that Whitman had seen the doctor several months prior to the event. At that time, Charley had told Dr. Heatly, among other things, that sometimes he thought "about going up on the tower with a deer rifle and start shooting people." The University held a press conference about Whitman's visit to Dr. Heatly's office, and the doc himself explained that Whitman's threat was not specific to any person and thus he did not consider the boy to be a danger to society, blah, blah, blah. I have no idea whether this guy could have saved Whitman -and thus dozens of others - but I knew that there was one other non-specific threat out there he had not addressed. What would happen to the good doctor if the Mystery Man did something and my visit to him became public? I really didn't care about Heatly, but I didn't want that to happen.

Others looked for scapegoats. Why hadn't the Austin Police been ready for something like this? Why hadn't the University realized the Tower could serve this purpose? Why couldn't they take Whitman out from a helicopter early on? Why? Why? Why? As we stood out there exchanging conjectures, we didn't know half of the story yet.

When we did hear the details of how he killed his wife and then his mother, we felt heartsick. To know that he had encountered and murdered members of the Gabour family of Texarkana in the stairwell leading to the observation deck struck close to home. Every one of us had taken family to that deck to look out over the campus and Austin beyond. We were to take Tira there later that week. Whitman's killing of Edna Townsley, the brusque receptionist to the Tower's observation deck, made us weak in the knees. We knew her or we felt like we did. We may not actually have known Edna, but we all had encountered her or one of the other ladies who had us register our names as we entered the Tower deck. Whitman cracked the back of her head with the butt of his rifle. These deaths at close range were all the more difficult to take. The long-distance killing was frightening, but the two women in his life, the Gabours, and Edna were different. They were personal somehow, and we felt even more like any one of their deaths could have been ours.

We broke off the speculation and discussion around 10:00 PM. At this point I tried to get Janell to come to work with me, but she declined, of course. Tira would not feel comfortable there. That would be even scarier for a kid. Best to stay in the apartment where they would both be more secure. They would be all right — really. Walking out of that apartment door that night was so very hard. I knew that sleep would not come easily, if at all, when I got to work, so I planned to call Janell as soon as I got there. We could talk the night away. I never had to make that call because the phone in the Director's Office was ringing when I walked in the front door. I said a perfunctory good-bye to the cleaning crew as I let them out the door and then raced back to the phone. It was Janell.

"Listen to this," she said. At that she stretched the

phone to the window so I could hear the loud hammering sounds. Even from that distance and over the phone, the sound was deafening. It was constant, insistent, and angry.

"Has he gone over the edge?" she asked when she got back on the phone.

"I don't know. Do you want me to come home? I'll walk away right now if you need me," I said.

"Well, there's no sleeping tonight anyway, so the hammering can't bother us that much. If it stops or if anything happens, we'll call."

"If anything happens, call the police. Don't call me," I said.

"OK," she said.

For me, sleep was not an option. I thought seriously about going home despite what Janell had told me. Leaving my post and leaving the building unguarded worried me, but I was inclined to do it anyway. I resolved simply to call periodically to check on Janell and Tira. At 3:00 AM, Janell said to let it go. The hammering had not stopped and the jarring ring of the telephone bothered her as much as anything. Later she told me that the hammering never stopped, but she and Tira did drift off to sleep. In their hazy dreams the Mystery Man's hammering morphed into Whitman's shots. Each dreamed of being on the campus. Each was shot at and each would wake up momentarily, take in where the sounds were coming from, and then sleep again. The hammering may or may not have stopped. Both continued to hear it – and thus the shots – all night long.

I rushed home at 6:00 AM to find Janell and Tira asleep in one tiny bed. The hammering had stopped. The drive home through the empty Austin streets had been surreal. I fought off sleep. I left the radio on to help me stay awake and the Austin station that usually played rock and roll all day played Garner Ted Armstrong in the early mornings. That morning Garner Ted talked of Armageddon, the Final Days, and how Anglo-Saxons were direct descendants of the ten lost tribes of Israel. Coming the day after the Whitman shootings and a missed night of sleep, Garner Ted was less amusing than ominous. Racing through my mind was not Armageddon, however. It was how to resolve our Mystery Man dilemma. I had come to a firm conclusion.

I would take responsibility.

Chapter XX

Rear Window

"No, you absolutely cannot go with me," I insisted. "We have been over this."

"Take someone with you then," Janell insisted.

"No, there's no one. This is up to me. Don and Ray are gone for the rest of the summer. Tony has gone home and wouldn't help anyway. Mahmoud knows nothing about this and he's too smart to do it in any event. Besides, I should not endanger anyone else."

"Forget it then," Janell responded. "We did our best. The University, the police, no one would take us seriously. Let someone else deal with it."

"We have covered this, too, Honey. We might leave here safe and sound, but could we live with another Whitman?"

She shook her head no and I concluded: "I know I couldn't either. If I am not back in thirty minutes, call the police."

"Thirty minutes is an eternity," she replied.

127

That was true. In thirty minutes Mack Herring could drive from Odessa to Notress to kill Betty. In thirty minutes Soviet missiles could fly from Russia to Washington, DC. In thirty minutes, Charles Whitman could park his car, ascend to the Tower, bludgeon Edna Townsley, kill three members of the Gabour family and take his position on the Tower observation deck. In thirty minutes, anything could happen.

"I know," I said, "but not doing anything is not an option for me. I will be careful. If he starts shooting, I will get the hell out of there. The police will have to act then."

"How can this be?" she asked. "You are risking our future on this guy, and we just survived the Whitman shootings."

"I know. I am afraid," I said. "I am just not clever enough to know what else to do."

"I love you," she said. "You're my hero."

"I love you, too, Honey. When we have children, tell them that."

"I am not pregnant, Dummy, so if you want children, you are just gonna have to come back."

"Thirty minutes," I said. "Watch out the back window."

"As planned," she responded.

With that I kissed her, gathered myself, and walked out of the apartment. The events of the summer raced through my mind as I walked down the narrow stairs to the ground floor. The Whitman shootings, now a week past, seemed somehow unreal, while the Mystery Man was a part of the fabric of our lives. His hammering, once such a jarring and ominous presence, had become part of the night's background noise for us. Janell had to have it to go to sleep. I wanted it because I knew as long as he was hammering, I knew where he was and, more or less, what he was doing. For the past few nights, however, there had not been complete silence. This was the most disturbing sound of all.

At the bottom of the steps, I realized that I had to think through what I was about to do. I wasn't sure exactly how to approach the house. After all Houston McCoy and Ramiro Martinez, the guys who killed Whitman, had debated how to approach the Tower. Of course, they were professionals and they had guns. Nevertheless, I had to make some choices. Front door, back door. Make noise and flush him out? Use stealth and surprise him? What if he were dead? We had not heard a sound from him in days. Did he do himself in? What if he had booby-trapped the house? Would I be his first victim? I laughed at myself as I looked down at my right hand and realized that on the way out of the apartment, I grabbed the only weapon in my arsenal – a cracked Jackie Jensen baseball bat. At least, I thought, it may be of some use this year.

The back yard and stealth were my choices. It was broad daylight, so it was not going to be possible to be invisible. We wanted it that way. Janell and I had waited until the sun came up, but before 9:00 AM. His old pattern had been to leave after 9:00 AM. We wanted him to be there. We wanted it to be daylight so I could see and he would not have the advantage of knowing the interior of the house while I groped my way in the dark. But I wanted the element of surprise on my side. Thus, the stealth. I had donned my black Keds sneakers just for the occasion. I could get traction; I could walk more quietly; and I'd be ready if he wanted to play a little one-on-one basketball.

I exited the Rose at the same place Janell first saw him, by the narrow passage between the Frat house and the Rose's laundry room. That way I could not be seen from the back windows of the Victorian house for at least the 20-30 feet on the backside of the Rose. Then if I could get across his backyard over to a small shed out there, I could get thirty feet closer. Then it would just be a matter of making it to the back door quietly and without being seen. I figured that if he were in the attic, he would probably look out and away from his windows but not down to his own backyard. Then it'd simply be a matter of getting in the back door and then … what?

About then I kicked myself for not having asked Don or Janell details about what the house was like on the inside. A Marine, like Whitman, would never have failed to gather that kind of intelligence. Note to self: if you are ever drafted, get a desk job. I stood at the back corner of the Rose thinking about all this and it didn't dawn on me that while the Mystery Man could not see me, any early morning risers at the Frat house could. They just had to peer out the plate glass window and there I was. I glanced over, and there they were - two guys in jeans, wearing no shirts or shoes. They seemed to be eating cereal and the sight of me, back flat against the wall, baseball bat in hand, seemed more to amuse than alarm them. I made no gesture at all to them, and actually I was glad that someone else knew what I was doing. I just hoped the Mystery man could not see them watching me.

I took a quick look around the corner and glanced up at the top window. There was no glare and I could see no one there, so I walked quickly over to the shed in the house's back yard. Unfortunately a few boards and a rusty can were around the shed and try as I may I could not avoid stepping on them. *Was the sound too loud?* From there I could look back to the Rose and into our apartment's back window. There was Janell. The window was open while she sat at the windowsill, her head on her hands, looking out at the drama unfolding before her. We had practiced this early morning nonchalance for a few days before, so this day would not differ from the any other. We wanted to condition the Mystery Man to Janell's presence in the window the way he had conditioned us to his hammering. I needed her to be my eyes and ears as I approached the house. Sure all this seemed like Rear Window, but in that movie the girl, Grace Kelley, goes over to the madman's scary apartment while the guy, Jimmy Stewart, watches. I liked it this way better. I looked up at her and pointed to my ear? Hear anything? She nodded her head no. I pointed to my eye. No, she shook her head, she had not seen anything either.

I moved from the back of the shed to its side. From there I could dash onto the back porch. I did so quickly and quietly, but I didn't crouch and run. I walked as silently as I could. I was especially careful going up the three-step backstairs to the small porch. I wanted no noise to signal me as an intruder. I carefully pulled open the screen door and was happy that it opened easily and without much sound. That left the back door. Would it be locked? How could it be? He would have no key. But, wait, he could lock it when it was inside and unlock it as he left. That was in a modern house, I thought; these old houses require a key for both entry and exit. Just try it, Dummy, I thought. I did and it was open! Carefully I pushed the door open. As slowly and as quietly as I could, I pushed the back door open. It led to a kitchen. I was in. I looked back up to our apartment to alert Janell to the obvious. I was in and I was going up.

She was not there.

Chapter XXI

Welcome to the Fun House

Crazy time for a bathroom run, I thought. Oh well, she'll see I have gone in when she gets back. I closed the back door behind me out of habit. Almost immediately I thought I should leave it open in case I had to run back out that way. Still, it was shut. The inside of the house looked like my grandmother's place in Goreville, IL. It was in no way elegant. The kitchen was small. It had a large white porcelain sink with a divider; overhead cupboards with handles that were added in the 1940s and worn out by the 1960s, three-tier built-in shelves against the wall, an empty spot where a refrigerator once stood, and no place for a dishwasher. There was no sign that anyone had set foot in that room anytime recently. I stood in the wide kitchen door leading to the dining room and looked around the downstairs.

The clutter was amazing. How, I wondered, did debris blow into a house? Drive the oilfield roads in West Texas and you'll see paper, wet boxes, trash, cans and bottles collecting at the base of barbed wire fences stretching for miles. The wind and people's general disregard for the environment explain that, but what could explain this? Newsprint and butcher paper were strewn everywhere. The floors, the mantle over the fireplace, and, from what I could see, even the bottom of the stairs were covered. More pictures of women? No, smudges of dirt and wood splinters, but no pictures. I presumed there were wood floors, but I could not see them. The high ceilings, the long windows, and the built-in coat-rack in the foyer were uncovered, but everything else was papered over. There were twigs. Innumerable twigs were scattered on top of the papers. It was the Mystery Man's alarm system! Anyone walking across those papers would automatically step on the man-made noisemakers and alert the guy upstairs. If I took one step out of the kitchen, he could hear me.

But wasn't that the plan? Let him know we knew he was there? Janell and I had decided to intervene in his little psychodrama. Confront him or scare him before he did something really awful. Yes, but we wanted to do so without provoking him. Go into the house, tell him we were onto him, encourage him to get help or go home, appeal to whatever reason he had left. Don't crash into the attic asking to be shot or stabbed, however. We know you're there and we know you're stealing stuff in the neighborhood, so you had better come clean. A frightened kid might crumble. A Richard Speck might come after me, but I am a former Odessa Permian football player. Surely

I could outrun him and then surely the police would have to get involved then. What choices did we have left? What was I to make of this early warning system of twigs and paper? Assume the worst and expect him to shoot me? Figure that it meant he had an escape route from the attic to ground outside the house? What?

I tested it. I took a step. Snap. There was no way to climb over this stuff. Perhaps if I had a big broom, I could push it quietly out of the way. Assume a broom. I had none. Push it forward with my hands? How long would that take? I decided to clear the way with my foot. I would slide the debris away with the side of my foot and move slowly across the floor without actually lifting my feet off the floor. Would it work? Would it take too much time? Janell was to call the cops in thirty minutes. Would they burst in to find me as an intruder while the Mystery Man escaped out the attic window? Worse, had he left days ago and would they just find me and a totally clean attic? Why don't I just turn around and go home now?

The crash from the upstairs sounded like boxes of wooden toys falling to the floor from an unsteady closet shelf. At first I turned to run away, but the backdoor was shut and it stuck when I tried to pull it open. Or maybe I pushed instead of pulled. I don't know, but it didn't open. Then I heard moaning sounds. They were low and almost inaudible, but they were moans. I decided to go upstairs. Fast. I ran over the papers and twigs and up the stairs. I didn't hear *Psycho* music in my head and I didn't fear getting shot or stabbed. I didn't know what I would find up those stairs but fear didn't play into my emotions. There may have been danger. There may have been none. But the time for speculation, worry or anxiety was over. Getting to the top of the stairs as fast as I could was all that mattered to me.

The paper and twig trail led all the way to the top. I took two or three steps at a time, and I am sure I made a lot of noise. When I got to the second floor, I could see the attic opening was covered. An old folding chair stood strategically below the opening, and it was obvious that the Mystery Man used the chair to ascend and descend the attic. I could hear the moaning more clearly now. The guy was in pain directly above me. I stood on the chair and pushed up on the attic door. Something heavy lay on top of it. I strained to push it up, but I could only raise it an inch or two. The bat! Somehow I had forgotten that I even had it. I checked my hand and then I looked around and it was gone. Quickly I raced back downstairs and there it was on the floor half way between the kitchen and the foyer. I retrieved it and went back to the chair. It was hard, but with the bat, I pushed the attic cover up and off. The Mystery Man had put a box with something heavy over the cover, but I managed to push it off. Throwing the bat aside, I pulled myself up to the attic. The moaning had stopped.

The only light in the attic was the sun's and it came in a solitary small window, but I could see that the Mystery

Man was lying on the attic floor with a noose around his neck. Some sort of contraption – a makeshift scaffold? – had collapsed around him. The roof beam above him had not held his weight. He lay hurt and stunned but he was not dead. I had come into his house the very moment that he had chosen to hang himself.

I couldn't see well and I didn't know what to do, but I loosened the thick rope from around the kid's neck. He looked even paler and considerably skinnier than Janell had described. Making sure that he was still alive, I lay his head back and went over to the attic opening. As I started to climb down it, a flashlight blinded my eyes.

"Mr. Williams, are you all right?" Detective Cooper and two uniformed cops were there. Janell had called them. Just as I was about to enter the backdoor of the house, the Mystery Man opened his window and gestured to Janell. He seemed to be making the signal for hanging someone, a tilt of the head sideways, a hand movement tugging on an imaginary rope, his tongue thrust out. She yelled out but I didn't hear. She called the cops. She thought I was to be the hangee. He didn't even know I was coming.

The cops didn't have to save his life because his suicide attempt failed and his fall from the scaffold simply bruised him and knocked the wind out of him. He would, in fact, recover quickly form his physical trauma. His emotional scars took much longer.

I found the note. In scratchy handwriting, he said:

Dear Mom,

I tried. I really tried. I failed and you and dad
don't tolerate failure.

Good-bye. I love you.

Your son.

He signed his name, but I am not telling you that. Janell was right. He was a lost, confused, and sad kid. His hard-charging doctor dad had pushed him all his life. The little West Texas town where he grew up did not have challenging schools, so his stellar academic record there meant nothing at UT. His first semester at UT the prior fall, he flunked Biology, Chemistry, and stopped going to the other classes. In fact he stopped going to any classes the second semester, and he stopped contacting his parents frequently. Unbelievably, they never tried contacting him at school. A brief note at the beginning of the summer told his parents that he was enrolling in summer school, but they never reacted to his grade reports or to the lack of a summer school tuition bill. They just abandoned him.

He chose the house to live in as a sanctuary. He could not bring himself to go home, get a job, or try again. He hammered away for no good reason at wooden blocks he found in the attic. He had placed most of them on the attic cover. The scaffold was a last minute decision, and in fact he was not much of a carpenter. He never intended to take his own life but he grew more and more depressed. When Whitman started shooting people, it drove him deeper into a remorseful state. He had gone through a phase when he hated his father and then one when he hated his mother – he symbolically killed them by cutting up pictures of "oh so glamorous people" – but after Whitman, he just hated himself. He wanted just to be left alone, but he knew Janell was watching him. He watched her as well. She was a "pretty lady," and he found her interest in him somehow comforting but confusing. After all, she seemed never to report him to the police.

We found out all these things from the police and then later from him. Janell and the Mystery Man corresponded for years afterwards. He needed lots of help, and eventually he also got out of West Texas. Last we heard he was selling men's clothes in a small town somewhere in Central Texas. He was good at it. When we moved back to Texas from Washington, DC in 1970, we waited way too long to contact the Men's Store where he was working. The word we got was that he had moved to the Houston area to manage a store there. Someday, we thought, we'll look him up in Houston.

Some day never came, but we will be forever connected.

CHAPTER XXII

IT'S A FAMILY THING

The summer of 1966 changed Janell and me forever. In a sense that was when I came back to life as a feeling person. From the time my cousin Betty died until then, I was angry, frustrated, and afraid. Mostly afraid. I was afraid of failure, afraid of other people, afraid of the future. Despite making excellent grades, I worried that I couldn't make it through UT, transferred that to worry about graduate school, and compounded that with worry about finances. I shut myself off from everything that had sustained me as a young person – family, church, friends, or any activity other that studying. I thought I had to do that. As a result, my beautiful wife moved in with damaged goods. I had become someone who thought he was being responsible to his wife and his future while actually becoming someone who sacrificed the present and lost any sense of why he was working hard and giving up so much. In the thirty-sixth year of my teaching career, I have met myself in so many college students. I try to deflect them from compulsive over-achieving above all things. I am sure that every one of them can quote me on what I think the key to happiness is in their lives: find something you love and get someone to pay you for it.

In that attic with the Mystery Man, it hit me. He and Whitman were victims of misplaced expectations. Each had succumbed to demons far worse than mine. I thought, as I had with my cousin, Betty, what is so awful in your life that you wish to end it? I did not know his full story then, but the Mystery Man's note talked about failure and how his parents could not tolerate it. Whitman's father considered the boy a failure at making money. My dad did as well, but it also hit me that these fathers also had their own fears. All of them did and, when I became a father, I would as well. I recalled that my reaction to Betty's death was two-fold. No, I protested, she didn't really want to die. She just asked that boy to kill her to get attention – the boy's and ours. My second reaction was: why would she allow her father to dictate her life? Why did she let him make her miserable? You want out, just get out. You don't have to give up on life. That is why I left Odessa and left home without approval. To hell with what my dad wanted me to do. I would pursue my own path. However, I became my own worst critic. My As were not enough; my efforts were not sufficient; I needed to work harder. The Mystery Man and Charles Whitman did not have the capacity to go their own path. I did, but I made it unnecessarily difficult. I actually became worse than my own father.

Whitman's and the Mystery Man's pathologies were much more complicated than I can imagine. Either one or both of them may have been bipolar. They may have had genetic disorders. Who knows? What drives someone to suicide or self-destruction? Nevertheless, in that old house on that day in August, I recognized exactly what was happening to the Mystery Man as quickly as I figured out what was happening on the Drag that awful day. I knew instantly what the crash in the attic was. I knew he had done something to himself. Don't ask me how I knew, but I knew. I felt responsible for him. I felt in 1961 that I had not done enough to help my cousin. In 1966 I was not going to walk away from either the Mystery Man's internal struggles or my sense of connection to other people. I stopped thinking about myself the instant I heard that crash. To a considerable extent I did the same at 24th and Guadalupe when I told people to turn away from the University as Whitman shot people from the Tower. Nothing I have done since that summer has ever made me more proud, but I would never claim to be a hero or ever predict what I would do confronted with another such crisis.

Charles Whitman and the Mystery Man saved my marriage. It's not that simple, of course, and maybe it would have happened anyway. Janell got her man back as a result of that summer. Everything from Yahtzee to bullets to suicide made me realize the importance of connection to people. I meet young students every year who demonstrate that they have not learned this lesson. Their resumes, their grades, their status, their self-worth is the end all of their existence. I anger many of them and I anger their parents by telling them that they have largely missed the point. How well will you connect to other people? What values will you live by? How connected can you be to others and the things that bring you passion? Parents, and there are evidently millions of them, who drive and humiliate their kids to succeed, accomplish, perform, excel, but not to connect, are creating monsters. These people may not commit suicide or take a deer rifle to the Tower, but they will hurt others – and themselves.

It's parenting. My parents, Betty's parents, Mack's parents, Charley's parents, the Mystery Man's parents, they all crafted who we'd become. So did Janell's and these poor, uneducated, unsuccessful people loved, respected and nurtured her into one fine person. They were not perfect and she is not perfect, but she provided me an incredible model for putting things into perspective. If you don't make an A in that class, you'll survive. If grad school doesn't work out, we'll get by. If that job doesn't pan out, another will come along. Your mood or your anxiety cannot be allowed to destroy our happiness and especially not our children's happiness. Your purpose in life is not to go as far or as high as you can go, it is to create a healthy environment for the people who love you.

Note to self: hang onto this woman. It is extremely ironic that the events of the summer of 1966 would lead to all this. Like I said, I vowed to focus my memories of

August 1 on the people who survived, but lessons come to one from the oddest angles and the most unlikely sources. I'll also never forget what Janell said to me on the trip from Austin to Washington, DC. After essentially laying out the thoughts I had about the "meaning of all these events," I opined that I was glad they were all over and that I was sure that life would not hold anything crazier or more dangerous than the events of the summer of 1966. We had no more lessons to learn.

She replied: "Oh, I don't know. Let's be open to what's in store. You never know, the adventures may have just begun."

As usual, she was right and I was wrong.

CHAPTER XXIII

LOOKING BACK

When I left Austin in the summer of 66, the nation was embroiled in an increasingly unpopular war overseen by a president from Texas who had been selected by the American people in large part because we thought him more capable of dealing with national security than his opponent. My, how times have changed. When I returned to Austin to put the finishing touches to this book in December 2005, politics were far from my mind, however. With the publication and subsequent hubbub surrounding my first book, *Washed in the Blood*, friends and even some family began asking me why I was so willing to write such personal, revealing stories. Why not let things rest? Why expose yourself? One writes because one must, I suppose. Write what you know, we have been told by English teachers, authors, and journalists. Write to discover truths. That's what I want to do, and if I happen to stumble on any while I am telling these little stories, I hope it isn't all by accident. Grander, more complex, more imaginative tales can be told, but they are not mine to tell. I think I write because I am fortunate to have known a lot of interesting and unimportant people from whom I have learned a lot.

Shel Hershorn is one of those people, but I am not sure I can call him unimportant. Someone who worked for three decades as an award-winning photojournalist. The guy who took the images for Life Magazine of both the Charles Whitman aftermath and the trial of boy who killed my cousin. That sort of person is important, though he may not be famous beyond aficionados of his first love photography or his current love, furniture making. But visiting Shel by phone on several occasions made me nostalgic for a life and a time that I had never experienced. Here was a guy who also left home early but to join the military at 17 and almost by accident fell into taking pictures. As a "photog," he then led a life of adventure, wine, and, at one time, women, and he met some of the most colorful characters of Texas in the booming post World War II era. Oddly his most famous image is not one of a person, though his photographs of people show folks like himself – learned through experience, practical, clever, or world wise –in ways few others have. Thumb through old copies of Life or newspapers in Texas in the 50s and 60s and you'll see Shel's indelible mark on our perceptions of reality.

But the cover of Life on August 12, 1966 probably made the biggest impression on all of us. There was the Tower of the University of Texas as seen though a store window with two gaping bullet holes in it. The Tower is depicted from the ground view of a potential victim and one can only conclude from looking at the Tower from this vantage point and from this distance that this inanimate object is ...evil. Perhaps it looks only menacing but it is definitely not the symbol of football victories and proud graduates. To some of us the Tower will always have this feel, even in broad daylight on sunny days.

Shel knew he had something the second he entered that store and saw the Tower from that perspective. He took several images and he tried several perspectives, always shooting at an upward angle to expose the full height and majesty of the Tower. It was clear that the shot "worked" and that he had something, but immediately after shooting it Shel realized that he also had a problem. Standing outside the store with camera at the ready was a UPI photographer. UPI prints stories – and pictures – on a daily basis, while Life went to press but once a week. Shel could well be scooped even though he had taken the image first. With only a second's hesitation, Shel kicked in the window and turned to the startled store owner.

"Life Magazine will pay for that," he said almost casually.

Shel saved his scoop and preserved the image in color for Life to use in 1966 and for me to put on the cover of this book. I thank him for that and I hope someday to make it to Galina, New Mexico where to this day he is making beautiful hand-made furniture for lovers of true craftsmanship. In December, 2005, I visited the American Museum of History on the campus of the University of Texas to view Shel's pictures and to select the ones that we would display in this book. Linda Patterson, the librarian in charge of the section that houses photographic images, escorted me into a viewing room. Looking at those images took me back to that time and it made me wonder even more about the guy who took them.

Maybe it takes someone born in the forties to admire the creativity and moxie of a guy like Shel. Someone who could move from farming to photography to furniture making impresses the hell out of me. Could a mere PhD in International Politics with a lifetime of teaching and writing ever acquire such practical arts? My dad would have appreciated Shel and he would have admired what he accomplished, but two years before Dad died, he asked his tenured, full professor son how he ever expected to support a family "just teaching."

Times have changed. In my dad's and Shel's day, a high school diploma would suffice. An autoworker, small time entrepreneur, or newspaper shutterbug could make it on wits, a meager formal education, or "lessons learned" from the Depression or the "Big War." Today a college degree is de rigeur and certain "career paths" seemingly guarantee success. The Mystery Man's parents saw this future and demanded him to pursue medical school. For decades as an undergraduate professor, I have encountered students whose whole lives seemingly turned on becoming a doctor, lawyer, or diplomat. There were, simply put, no other options. Never mind the stories I told them of college drop outs who started their own companies. Never mind the slew of lawyers, doctors, or mid-level diplomats who felt trapped in careers, once attained, that didn't seem quite as glamorous, fulfilling, or secure as they once did. As one student recently told me: "My whole life is about becoming a doctor!" Now, if she could only pass Chemistry.

Arguing about this is no use. "But, Shelly, you worked incredibly hard and you made it" is often the response. "Why should I give up? Besides, my parents won't let me." But giving up is never the advice I give. "Do what you love and find someone to pay you for it," is what I actually say. That will be the key to your success and more importantly to your happiness. "Easy for you to say," responds the student, "you got your PhD." Trust me, even getting a PhD and pursuing what you really love will not make it an easy path. No path guarantees success, much less happiness. Nevertheless, students and especially parents for the most part seem to send their kids to college with "the path" already selected and the rewards already deposited in the 401K. I see in the students' motivations what I saw in me in 1966: **fear of failure**. That fear emanates from the culture, from peer pressure, and definitely from their parents' motivations and expectations (and their fears that junior won't make it). These are real and legitimate concerns. It's tough today without a college education and guys like Shel or my dad and their wives don't much exist any more. The cultural assumption of success without a college education is disappearing. A formal education is necessary, I admit, but the notion of a guaranteed path is equally unrealistic. Find what you love and get someone to pay you for it. Even at twenty, you can think for yourself.

Shel's life and work alone didn't inspire the above thoughts. Walking around the campus of the University of Texas always brings my thoughts back to why I ever came there in the first place. It was also delicious irony that on Friday, December 2, 2005, I was there to meet another educator. Why should that be ironic? It's because the guy I was supposed to meet was a best-selling true crime author who had, in my opinion, written the definitive book on Charles Whitman. He had also written several books about serial killers and other modern monsters. I had built up an image and back story for Gary Lavergne long before I met him. His book, *A Sniper in the Tower*, had been my constant companion as I wrote this book. I cared not about the controversies of why Charley had done what he did or who should get credit for killing him. My interest was in his relationship to his dad and how that relationship contributed to his fury and his discontent. Lavergne paints an incredibly vivid picture of this relationship and of all the events and personalities of the Whitman Saga. In my imagings I pictured Lavergne as an old newspaper man who wrote true crime for a living and who brought his flair for research and writing to bear on a story ripe for the telling.

I had to work up my nerve to contact this guy. I had written another book that some called true crime and some called a memoir, but I was not a professional writer of true crime. I didn't know all the ends and outs of police work, and I didn't know the case histories of murderers and the people who pursued them. I assumed that Lavergne did and that a call from me to him would be like Don Knotts calling Sam Spade. Finally, on a winter day in Washington, DC, I walked into my office on Massachusetts Ave and simply Goolged the name Gary Lavergne. I could not believe my eyes. This was no Sam Spade. This was a Mr. Chips or perhaps the guy who processed the students through the admissions' office where Mr. Chips taught. Gary Lavergne is the Director of Research at the Office of Admissions at…the University of Texas. His office is in the Tower. He is a fellow educator and he has worked with admissions offices, with those hated standardized tests we all endure, and with research on the kinds of people who do or don't get into the University and who do or don't make it in that environment. He has over thirty years of educational experience and he is well trained in History and Political Science. In short, he is a colleague. How he ever turned his many historical skills into writing about mass murderers and serial killers he explains in the afterword of this book.

In short, calling Gary Lavergne was like calling an old friend and, initially unbeknownst to me, we in fact had a mutual old friend in the person of Nan Davis, Vice President for Admissions at Austin College. Austin College had also opened the door for me with Shel Hershorn since Shel had spent several days on its campus in the '70s taking pictures for a development project. With both Gary and Shel, it had seen like old home week, but walking into the Tower at 11:00 AM on that Friday in December was an odd and even creepy sensation. It was the first time I had ever reentered that building since before Charles Whitman went on his rampage. Walking across campus to get to the Tower, I had to remark to myself that the UT students of today dress more like they did in 1966 when I left than in 1962 when I entered. The social revolution that began while Janell and I were at UT left a permanent mark. The faces in 2005 were also more diverse than even in 66. I was certain that Mr. Lavergne had had something to do with their admission to the great University.

An hour after I walked into the Tower alone, Gary and I exited the building to walk around the Mall in front of the Tower. It was a sunny day; it was 12:00 PM; and students crisscrossed the Mall without glancing upwards. Gary and I were on a bit of a mission that day, however. He was going to show me the evidence of Whitman's acts and I was going to show him where I had encountered Charley Fingernails and where friends of mine had been when the shootings started. "Where you were" when Whitman shot at folks is a common game Texans play. Anyone from Austin or any UT student, past or present, has a story about herself, his uncle, an old friend who was there or nearly there. Everyone has a story, but no one can explain why it happened. Kinky Friedman wrote a "ballad" about it; Lavergne wrote a book about it; and TV shows have recounted it, but no one has ever been able to explain why.

"Do you think he did it to get back at his daddy?" I asked Whitman's biographer as we walked across the Mall. In *Sniper* Lavergne chronicles Whitman's troubled relationship with his dad. He talks of the traumatic breakup of his parents' marriage; and he reports that of the letters Whitman left, only one, to his father, has not been made public. To call his relationship with his dad "troubled" appears to be a vast understatement. In Whitman's own words, he says that he murdered his own mother and wife so they would not have to live with the shame of being related to a mass murderer (and to save them from the awfulness of life's vicissitudes). Whitman clearly wanted his dad to live with that shame.

"It's impossible to pinpoint and exact reason," Lavergne responded, "but boiling it all down, yes, it seems that shaming and hurting his dad was a strong motivation. After all, this was the guy who pushed him to be an Eagle Scout, to accomplish so much, but seemingly to do it not for the son's development but for his own personal gain. Charles turned all back on his dad and punished him for hurting Charlie and his mom."

Gary and I both know that Whitman's story is not unique, that his relationship with his dad is not "sufficient" to explain his actions. Even before I could, Gary noted that my relationship with my dad was not dissimilar to Whitman's with his father. "Not every troubled relationship ends with mass murder," Lavergne said. "Such relationships do not cause murder or we would have them all around us everyday. Sometimes people choose to do evil things." Neither of us knew what our Psychology colleagues would say about this conclusion, but it is one we share. Now he had a question for me. "Take the Mystery Man in your book, Shelly, was he real? He chose to turn against himself, not against the world. What do you think of his outcome?"

The Mystery Man is real, but the events in the last chapters of the book are fictionalized. Janell and I never solved the mystery of who he was or where he came from. The person I saved from suicide; the person who went on to sell clothes; the person whose parents banished him for not being a successful Pre Med is real, but "he" is many different students, both male and female, I have encountered over thirty-five years of college teaching. He's the student whose parents have cut off all ties with him because he's gay. He's the young woman whose father threatened to divorce her mother because the daughter dared even to take a class not related to medical studies. He's the guy whose dad cut him off financially for deciding not to become a lawyer. He's the two people, former students, who in the last year confessed to me that I had intervened in their lives just at the moment they were contemplating suicide. The "real" Mystery Man never revealed himself.

He hammered all night after Whitman shot at us; he lived in the abandoned house next to us; he cut up pictures of women; he stole from us and the Minit Mart, but he was never unmasked. Janell's and my efforts to get the police, the University, the psychiatrist, and the neighbors to help this guy were absolutely real, but we moved away before any resolution could occur. If you are that Mystery Man, we wish you well and we hope no harm came to you or others.

I write because I am a teacher. When I was at the University of Texas, I declared to one of my professors my intention to become a high school teacher. He scoffed at my plan and commented that there was no intellectual challenge in that. He said that the pay, the bureaucracy, and the low intellectual stimulation would make high school teaching a "waste of my University education." I succumbed to that pressure and decided to go to grad school at one of the premier research universities in the US, but I still wanted to teach. When I graduated at the top of that University program, I accepted a job at a small liberal arts college in Sherman, Texas, so I could teach. Upon hearing of my decision to take this position, the Head of the Foreign Languages Department at Johns Hopkins School of Advanced International Studies, confronted me in the hallway and virtually spit out her charge: "How dare you insult a great university like Johns Hopkins by going to some Church College in Texas that no one has ever heard of!" This time I did not yield. I turned my back on her and

I marched into my mentor's office, Dr. Robert Osgood, the University's most prestigious professor.

"Have I insulted Johns Hopkins by taking this position?" I asked him.

"Two questions. Do you want to teach and will Austin College be a good place to do it?" he responded.

"You know I do and I think it will," I said.

"Then do what you love and let Austin College pay you for it," said the man who had become my real father.

And for the next thirty-six years that's exactly what I did.

AFTERWORD
Living With "Charley Fingernails"
An Afterword by Gary M. Lavergne, Author,
Sniper in the Tower
© 2007 Gary M. Lavergne, all rights reserved

I

During the summer of 1966, I was a skinny, ten-year-old Cajun boy growing up in Louisiana. My father had just been elected Chief of Police in our hometown.

My dad seldom watched television, and so I distinctly remember the hot summer day when I saw him, standing armed and fully-uniformed, staring at the small black and white screen in our little living room. The scene was a skyscraper I thought was the Louisiana State Capitol, and from an observation deck, just like the one in Baton Rouge, came gunshots and puffs of smoke. The date was August 1, 1966.

"Nolan, is that in Baton Rouge?" my mom asked.

"No, that's in Texas. Sooner or later those boys [policemen] are gonna fix him. He's not coming down alive," he said, before he realized he was watching the news and it was already over—and he was right.

What he said next has stayed with me: "This is not good. We gonna see more of this."

The Charles Whitman story was the first news story I ever really paid attention to. It was the first topic I sought to read about. The Life magazine cover with the bullet hole in the storefront window riveted me every time I went to Thibodeaux's Barber Shop for a haircut. I read the Texas Sniper story, stared at the pictures, and even considered stealing the magazine.

I can't think of another newsmaker that has kept my interest for as long as Charles Whitman, the character Shelly Williams calls "Charley Fingernails." I was never obsessed, but since the summer of 1966, every time I saw that iconic yearbook picture of the young, crew-cut, blue-eyed, blonde ex-Marine, I immediately recognized him as the sniper.

My direct experience with Texas had been limited to occasional trips to Houston and Dallas. I had never been to Austin. But then I read Robert Caro's brilliantly written book, The Path to Power.

> The Hill Country was a trap—a trap baited with grass... And from every new hill they climbed, the hills stretched away farther; according to these early settlers, every time they thought they were seeing the last range of hills, there would be another crest, and when they climbed it, they would see more ranges ahead, until the hills seemed endless—the Hill Country.

So, in December of 1987, when my brother-in-law told

me he was planning to fly his Cessna to Austin, Texas to visit his parents, I asked to go along. I wasn't giving much thought to Charles Whitman at the time; my first trip to Austin was to see the Hill Country.

When Austin came into view from the Cessna, I remember seeing the city's skyline and what was unmistakably the State Capitol. But my attention was ultimately drawn north to the Tower of The University of Texas. There was something magnetic about the structure that, as former UT President Larry Faulkner once described, "... looks down on some of the most valuable possessions of Texas."

And the image of the blonde, crew cut, all-American boy came back to me.

I never imagined that two years later I would be offered a job in Austin. I've worked for ACT, the College Board, and since September 2000 for the Admissions Office at The University of Texas at Austin as the Director of Admissions Research and Policy Analysis.

The ACT and SAT jobs required extensive travel, and from 1989 to 2000 I spent an average of ninety nights each year in hotels. I soon tired of HBO and Pay-Per-View movies. My life on the road became a search for something good to read.

On December 29, 1993, while home with my two sons I remember watching an episode of a series called American Justice. Bill Kurtis narrated an installment on the subject of mass murder. Criminologists like James

Alan Fox and Jack Levin analyzed and commented on the characteristics and profiles of mass murderers. Charles Whitman was central to the episode. I told my boys all about the 1966 UT Tower tragedy, and the next day I went to a bookstore in search of a responsibly written, competently researched book on that monstrous crime. It was then I discovered that none had ever been written. I said to myself, "Well, hell, I'll write one."

Whether I like it or not, I have been living with "Charley Fingernails" ever since.

II

It took me over three years to write *A Sniper in the Tower.* The breakthrough was when the head of the robbery/homicide division at the Austin Police Department brought me up to a third floor evidence room vault and showed me three old boxes labeled "Whitman." Whitman's notes, his diaries, pictures from his camera as well as police crime scene photographs, all of the Austin Police Department reports, Texas Department of Public Safety Intelligence Reports, and FBI files were in those three boxes. After nearly thirty years it was all still there, as if the case was still active.

Those boxes were an historian's dream. Today, unrecorded telephone conversations and deleted e-mail make oral history a necessary evil, but even today, non-fiction writers who know what they are doing will always give preference to official contemporaneous documents over the aged recollections of witnesses.

Sniper was the first of three crime/criminal justice

books I've published since 1997. Additionally, I've investigated in depth several other murders I considered but didn't write about. In every case there were conflicts between eyewitnesses and other eyewitnesses, eyewitnesses and documentation, eyewitnesses and forensic science, and even eyewitnesses and themselves.

That was but one reason why I only interviewed three people for Sniper in the Tower. The older the crime the less dependent a writer should be on witness interviews. This was an old crime, and since 1966, all of the survivors and eyewitnesses had been bombarded with thirty years of questions and other people's stories about what happened that day. Some of the stories they absorbed were accurate and just as many were utter nonsense. Once on a flight to Dallas, I was looking over Sniper in order to decide what passages to read at a book signing. The person next to me, not knowing I was the author of the book, saw the cover and took great pleasure in telling me that he was an ambulance driver that day and that he was instrumental in rescuing some of the wounded. "My partner and me kept on going even after Whitman blew out the back windshield and the 'bubble' off top of the ambulance," he said. It never happened. I've had others tell me, in great detail, about how they ran for their lives into buildings like the Harry Ransom Center, which did not exist in 1966. Some have regaled me with how they were good friends with Charley Whitman. One said he grew up with Whitman in Texas, when in fact, Whitman had grown up in Florida.

Many of those who claim to have been Whitman's friends say they find it impossible to believe he could have done what he did, while others, who claimed to have known him equally well, saw him as Shelly Williams' "Charley Fingernails." I've had UT alums tell me about their experiences in formal classes they had with Whitman—that he never took. About half remember him as a brilliant student—the others recall him taking hours to do calculations that should have taken a few minutes. What is the historian to believe? Well, the transcript, a contemporaneous official legal document, gives us definitive answers. At the time of his death Charles Whitman's official overall grade point average was about a 1.9 on a 4.0 scale. Case closed. Some of the teachers who remember him fondly and said he was a good student didn't give him very good grades.

For the historian, documents are always preferred, and the more the better. Really good non-fiction writers interested in producing a definitive story usually have to closely examine tens of thousands, or even hundreds of thousands of documents. It is often daunting and overwhelming, but the best advice I have ever received as a writer was from best-selling author Gerald Posner, who said: "You can't be afraid of paper."

Contrary to cop show dramatizations, it is extremely rare for police officers to jeopardize their cases and risk losing their jobs and pensions for falsifying a report. They also risk indictment, trial, and prison. For adjudicated crimes, trial transcripts are far better than any author interview because in court the witness is under oath and if he lies he can be charged with perjury. What greater incentive is there for someone to tell the truth? Moreover, a judge assures the relevancy of the questions, which are posed by trained attorneys during direct and cross-examination. A writer has no such leverage with a person he interviews and can never hope to match the majesty of the setting.

And the story won't change in twenty, thirty, or forty years.

It matters not that the eyewitnesses are sincere; most of them certainly are, but anyone who has ever listened to parents, grandparents, and fishermen knows that even those who love us tell stories that are organic: They change and grow with time.

III

The Austin Police Department file completely changed my preconceptions about the case. Those who say that from the start I was determined to make Charles Whitman a monster do not know me, because precisely the opposite is true. Before I got my hands on those papers I had accepted the theory that the brain tumor discovered during his autopsy triggered a seizure, of sorts, that overrode his ability to both control himself and discern the difference between right and wrong. Other Whitman apologists advance the "amphetamine psychosis" theory: that his abuse of Dexedrine brought about a psychotic episode. Then, there are those who advance his prior military indoctrination as the culprit: he was trained to kill. Other explanations include the fact that he was broke and had no immediate prospect for success, his parents were separated, his marriage was in shambles, he was taking too heavy a schedule at UT, and he had been spanked often as a child by an overbearing and dangerously surly father. These are all terrible things that anyone with common decency would not wish upon anyone else. They are also common on all college campuses. Rosa Eberly, a rhetorician at Penn State, in a journal article saying she doesn't want anyone to discuss "evil" because she doesn't know what it is (making her a rhetorician calling for censorship), conjectures that the fact that he faced these problems simultaneously might explain what he did. She should spend more time with her students: who among them, or us, has the luxury of dealing with one problem at a time? These conditions may tell us why Whitman was angry and why he wanted to die, but they do not provide absolution for murder any more than jealousy excuses a delusional husband for killing his innocent (or guilty) wife. Such convoluted logic is consistent with saying a woman's attractiveness and sexy dress changes a perpetrator's crime of rape into a "disorder."

Anyway, I ultimately concluded, and later the FBI's premier profiler, John Douglas, would agree in his book *Anatomy of Motive*, that "[Whitman's] actions speak for themselves." Any cause-effect theory, whether organic (brain tumor), chemical (amphetamine psychosis), or psychological (military training or child abuse), embracing the idea that Charles Whitman's judgment or free will was impaired, is not consistent with what he DID.

And we know, beyond not just reasonable, but any doubt, what he did, and how and when he did it. Sworn statements in the Austin Police Department files on Charles Whitman make it possible for competent investigators to reconstruct Whitman's activities during the forty-eight hours prior to the sniping in the Tower. During that period no significant amount of time is unaccounted for. He engaged in controlled, thoughtful, serial decision-making in a correct order to accomplish a goal. Nothing he did remotely appears undisciplined or random. Indeed, if a commando had been assigned to do the same thing, he would have assembled much the same arsenal, packed the same supplies, and behaved the same way.

And if, as was suggested by a forensic psychiatrist on "A&E's Biography," that his tumor might have affected the amygdala, which is believed to be related to rage, when did this rage or mental breakdown begin? Was he under the control of a tumor or drugs or in a state of rage when he went to a convenience store to buy the canned goods he intended to eat while on the deck? Right about that time he had lunch with his wife and mother at a cafeteria. He had begun his plans for their murder but didn't kill them there? Is that not control? Or did this loss of control begin with a trip to Academy Surplus where he bought the knife he used to kill them and the binoculars he had strapped around his neck while shooting fifty people? He was planning murder. If not, why did he buy these things? The Academy Surplus cashier didn't bother to check his I.D. because "he looked like such a nice boy."

Maybe the tumor or amphetamine psychosis kicked in when he bought his shotgun at Sears, where he asked the attendant about whether there was metal in the stock he intended to saw off later that morning. He wasn't in an uncontrolled rage when he asked that question. He didn't kill anybody at Chuck's Gun Shop. Whatever "disorder" he is reputed to have didn't seem to affect his shopping skills: He bought the right ammunition for appropriate weapons he intended to use and he even knew he was writing bad checks for all of it. For two days there is premeditation and no evidence of brain malfunction, psychosis, or rage. Is a writer to believe that Whitman happened to be alone with his mother, and separately alone with his wife, when these unavoidable rages surfaced and that he happened to have a large hunting knife with him?

Even if what is described above is remotely possible during rage or some other seizure or psychotic condition, was he out of control when the killings started and afterwards? After he beat and stabbed his mother to death he wrote "I have just killed my mother" in a note he left on her dead body. Then he forged a note with her name on it asking that she not be disturbed. If he was in a state of rage or under a seizure of some sort, or even if he was mildly delusional, how is it that one or all of those conditions disappeared a few minutes later when he calmly manipulated the doorman to keep people out of her apartment? When he called his mother's employer to tell them she would not be at work, he knew not to tell them she was dead because he had just murdered her—or did he really believe she was sick?

And when did this sinister force that took his

consciousness force him to kill his wife? The day before, his best friends had a pleasant time with him only moments after he typed what he INTENDED to do: "It was after much thought that I decided to kill my wife, Kathy, tonight after I pick her up from work at the telephone company." Only minutes after he typed that sentence those friends arrived unannounced and for the next sixty to ninety minutes he entertained them. Those friends drove away thinking he was as well-adjusted as they had ever seen him. For the entire visit, the note on the coffee table Whitman planned to leave on his wife's corpse already included the phrase, "...I don't want her to have to face the embarrassment my actions would surely cause her." What was she to be embarrassed about? How could he write that and not know what he was doing and that it was wrong?

Enough! I could go on and I haven't even gotten him to the Tower yet. Suffice to say that after three years of searching for what made this "all-American boy" a mass murderer, I could not delude myself any longer. How big a chump does a person have to be to swallow this "all-American boy" stuff?

On July 31st and August 1st of 1966, Charles Joseph Whitman was a cold and calculating murderer. Those who say they can't believe he would commit such a monstrous crime are only admitting that they didn't really know him. They never saw the "Charley Fingernails" side of Whitman Shelly Williams masterfully describes. But it was there; "a nice guy" doesn't shoot fifty innocent people.

My views are not as rigid as they may sound. I accept the limitations of my conclusions. None of us knows with absolute certainty that a meteor won't fall on our heads. We go about our business anyway; otherwise our lives will become paralyzed and meaningless. It is in that context, I maintain, that no one knows, with absolute certainty, why Charles Whitman became a mass murderer. However, I am satisfied and more than reasonably certain that had he been taken alive, in any court of law, Charles Whitman would have been found guilty of murder with malice, what we refer to today as capital murder, for the death of Austin Police Officer Billy Paul Speed. Prosecutors would have chosen that victim because at that time he was the only casualty (a police officer) that qualified Whitman for the death penalty. Whitman's defense attorney would first offer a guilty plea for a lesser murder charge to save his client from the electric chair. The Travis County District Attorney, then or now, would never entertain such an offer. The defense attorney would then have had no choice but to resort to an insanity defense. (He could not have argued that it was an accident, nor could he argue the right of self-defense.) A mediocre, junior Assistant District Attorney could have shredded that defense. Charley Whitman would have been sent to death row, to be spared the "chair" in 1972 by the U.S. Supreme Court's Furman v Georgia decision. Today, he'd either be alive in a Texas prison or dead and buried in "Peckerwood Hill" in Huntsville, Texas or the Hillcrest Cemetery in West Palm Beach, Florida—

depending on whether his dad would have been willing to spend the money to transport him there.

IV

A Sniper in the Tower: The Charles Whitman Murders was released in March of 1997, only three months after I started a new job at the College Board, and nearly four years before I joined the UT staff. (At the time of publication I had no connection to the University and had no friends of any kind on staff there.) All of the major dailies and trade magazines gave it good reviews. I was most gratified by the response of major players in academia, like Professor James Alan Fox of Northeastern University's School of Criminal Justice, who said it was "skillfully researched, documented, and analyzed." William Helmer, a senior editor of Playboy, an author of several crime books, and most importantly, an eyewitness who had more than a passing knowledge of the Tower shootings, said it was "cool and balanced." Neal Spelce, the dean of Austin reporters, who probably knows more about this incident than anyone, called it "a stunning achievement."

I am proud of my books and I have no regrets, but since March of 1997, I've had to live with Charley

Fingernails. I still get phone calls and e-mails from readers, students, or researchers at least a few times each a week. On the occasion of school shootings like the tragedy at Columbine High School, or other instances of simultaneous mass murder like the "Day Trader" in Atlanta, or other sniping incidents like the "D.C. Sniper," I can easily get 60-80 e-mail a day for as long as the incident is in the news. Japan's first experience with mass murder, the subway poisonous gas murders, brought a television crew from Tokyo to my home. Nearly all of those who write and call me agree with my conclusion that Whitman was quite conscious of what he was doing.

There are two categories of the few who disagree: first are serious professionals who listen and think and arrive at a conclusion different than mine. They produce work I respect. A good example is Dr. Norman Rosenthal, the author of The Emotional Revolution. Dr. Rosenthal interviewed me extensively for the portion of his book that refers to Charles Whitman. Immediately, I knew that we were going to disagree over what he was going to write. But Rosenthal never got angry or personal; he was a real pro. During our dialogue I surprised him with an offer to make available everything I had in the way of files and other documents. He took me up on that offer and used much of what I sent him. I even annotated and marked items in order to save him time. His thoughtfully inscribed book is a valued part of my personal library. The point is that I am not afraid of those who disagree with me; I'll even give them information.

Those in the other category make it difficult for me to live with Charles Whitman; they are "kooks." They are very few in number, but they make more noise and waste a lot of my energy. Some of them need to get a life. A former librarian and archivist of the Austin History Center, a warm and delightful person I knew and assisted in the processing and cataloging of the Austin Police Department's Whitman file, discovered this group after the Center opened the files to the public. As I had warned her, she received a number of odd inquiries, and like me, she has had to deal with individuals who have an unhealthy obsession with Charles Whitman. One person, a complete stranger to me, told her that he was my close friend and had helped me write *Sniper*. Another person, who apparently took some offense at something in my book, spoke about me with such acidity that it "creeped her out." Still another openly spoke about how his obsession with Whitman ruined his marriage and cost him his job. On other occasions, major news organizations, like the New York Times, thought it best to alert me to callers they have had who bitterly resented the exposure I've received.

Even more ominous was a series of anonymous e-mails that started off with questions about Whitman's hair and eye color. I responded that Whitman had blonde hair and blue eyes. Then he asked me if I had ever seen a color portrait of Whitman. I said, "no."

"Well then how do you know his eyes were blue,"

he wrote in a surly and curt tone.

I responded that Whitman's driver's license had that information on it and was in his wallet at the time of his death. Then he said, "I have been searching all day all over the Internet trying to find out if blonde hair and [blue eyed people] have smaller skull thickness, but without luck. I hope you understand my dilemma."

Finally, I told him that I would not answer any more questions unless he submitted them by regular mail with his name and address. He replied "… could you please tell me if Charles Whitman had a Jewish background?"

Now it was my turn to be "creeped out."

Some other instances are tragically amusing. During the 1997 Texas Book Festival, a complete stranger came to me, and without introduction said, "Did you know Charles Whitman had a blood clot removed from one of his testicles? Do you think that might have had something to do with what he did?"

Persons masquerading as authors, attorneys, screenwriters, and producers (including one who claimed to me and others to be all of the above at one time or another) have been trying to get my attention since 1996. I won't give it to them.

I've had a Ph.D. candidate ask me if she could adapt presentations I've made on Whitman into a dramatic performance. And almost every semester since *Sniper* was released, a Radio, Television and Film major at UT Austin has chosen Whitman for their documentary or film project.

(I have a copy of each one I've appeared in and some are really quite good.)

My favorite encounter involving the Charles Whitman story occurred immediately after I appeared in a news program with Neal Spelce on KEYE-TV in Austin. Immediately after the piece aired the station's receptionist came to the set and said, "Mr. Lavergne, you have an urgent call. I'll transfer it to a phone in the kitchen." So, I immediately went to the kitchen. This is my best recollection of what was said:

"Mr. Lavergne, my name is - - - - and I am a psychic. I thought you should know that your book is not the whole story.

"Really," I said.

"You see, Charles Whitman called me on the morning of August 1st, and I wasn't home to answer the phone and talk to him. I know that if I had been there to answer the phone I could have prevented him from going to the Tower."

Not knowing how to respond, I said, "Did the person who took the message think Whitman sounded upset or distraught?"

"Oh, no. No one was home," she said.

"Telephones didn't have answering machines back in 1966—did they? How do you know he called?"

"I told you! I'm a psychic !" she said with great indignation.

Less amusing and more ridiculous are discussions

and postings on Internet sites like Wikipedia. One of my sons alerted me to the "Wiki" page on Charles Whitman because I seemed to be the center of a controversy of sorts. I checked it out. Wikipedia is an egalitarian asylum for truth and lies, competence and incompetence, and scholars and morons. At one point the "article" on Whitman didn't even have the word "murder" in it.

And finally, because I am still a teacher at heart, there are instances of sloppy scholarship involving Whitman that I find painful. On the Internet there is an essay entitled "Charles Whitman: The Amygdala and Mass Murder" in which Whitman is used as a "case study in amygdala-aggression." In the case study section alone there are thirteen serious factual errors, one of which is that before climbing the Tower Whitman called the police and asked to be arrested. At very least the conclusions are based on a seriously flawed, even non-existent, case study. Another example came to my attention during the fall of 2003. I received the following e-mail (which I edited for this essay):

Dear Mr. Lavergne,

I'm a neurologist in Oregon, and recently was listening to a college audiotape course on Psychology by the Department Chair of Psychology at - - - - - - - Medical School. In his argument that nobody is really responsible for what they do, he gave Charles Whitman as an example... He also stated that Whitman had "turned the gun on himself." As I recall, the tumor formed part of his insanity defense.

As the author of three crime books I've had to deal with some pretty unpleasant people. So, I've gotten very good at doing background checks on the people who contact me. (Some had a record of violent crimes.) I checked out the neurologist and he was legitimate—he was who he said he was. Once I gave the doctor the correct information he thanked me and added:

> *We are taught as Neurologists that it's extremely rare, if it happens at all, that complex partial seizures... produce GOAL-ORIENTED violent behavior, especially over a considerable period of time. (All-caps in original)*

In my third book, I covered a murder trial whereby the defendant used complex partial seizures and other brain damage as the ingredients of an insanity defense. Expert testimony in that trial established that the average duration of a complex partial seizure is twenty-nine seconds, and if it last much longer, the patient is in serious medical trouble.

One of my other books, *Bad Boy From Rosebud*, actually sold far more copies than *Sniper*. But I never had to live with the "Bad Boy" (Kenneth Allen McDuff) like I've had to live with "Charley Fingernails." It is too much to call Whitman apologists a cult, but he has a following; I cannot understand why. Before I give any lecture or make any appearance, I remind myself that this man murdered seventeen people and wounded another thirty-one. He devastated or ruined the lives of the loved ones of his victims. Those people were not murdered by the legend of a "crew-cut blonde-haired, blue-eyed, all-American boy." When I think of Charley Whitman—I think of Shelly Williams' Charley Fingernails. The more successful Summer of 1966 becomes the more likely it is that Shelly Williams will have to live with Charley Fingernails—as I have.

Debunking legends is not easy. *In The Dark Side of Camelot,* Seymour Hersh wrote that much of the John F. Kennedy idolatry was really "about the power of beauty... Many are still blinded today." On a much smaller scale, of course, that reminded me of some of the Whitman disciples I've had to deal with. If Charley had been ugly, or if they had seen Charley Fingernails instead of "Charles Whitman: All-American boy" this story would have been far less resilient.

Gary M. Lavergne
Cedar Park, Texas

The press conference, Shel Hershorn

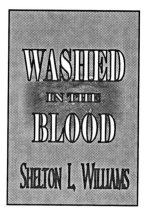

Washed in the Blood is a page-turning read about the time-
-early 1960s--and place--Odessa, Texas--during its rowdy oil
boom days when violence often rode the range. It is at once an
examination of local mores and foibles, piety and hypocrisy and
an inside-look at the famed 'Kiss and Kill' murder of a 17-year
old would-be actress, Betty Jean Williams, whose ghost is said
to haunt the Odessa High School campus to this very day. And
it is a courtroom saga starring the late trial super-lawyer, Warren
Burnett, along with a verdict that some think stood the blind
Goddess of Justice on her head. What Shelton Williams has
wrought here is worth both your time and your money.

Larry L. King, author, *The Best Little Whorehouse in Texas*

Available @ www.ZonePress.com

CPSIA information can be obtained
at www.ICGtesting.com
Printed in the USA
FFOW02n1604240118
44435387-44216FF

9 780977 755875